Back to Bethlehem

MODERN PROBLEMS IN THE LIGHT
OF THE OLD FAITH

By

JOHN H. WILLEY, Ph.D.

The Holiest among the mighty, and the Mightiest among the holy,
lifted with his pierced hands empires off their hinges,
and still governs the ages
—*Jean Paul Richter*

NEW YORK: EATON & MAINS
CINCINNATI: JENNINGS & GRAHAM

Copyright, 1905, by
EATON & MAINS.

TO
MY WIFE

CONTENTS

	PAGE
Prologue	5
The Survival of the Fittest	11
Environment	33
The Unity of the Race	55
The Development of the Race	79
Arrested Development—Militarism	101
The Philanthropy of God	127
The Service of God	153
The Law of Service	177
The Gospel of a Person	197
Jesus and the New Age	219
The Evolution of the Book	239
Epilogue	267

PROLOGUE

ALL roads lead to Bethlehem. The trunk lines of history, of science, of literature and of law, run straight across the field where the shepherds watched their flock by night, directly through the narrow, squalid streets of the relic makers, and converge upon a certain silver star in the heart of the little city of David. Out from this center and along these radii have come the things that have brought sunrise to the world.

More and more as the years pass and our intellectual horizon broadens must Jesus of Bethlehem be reckoned with. The scientist with his lenses, the critic with his particles, the antiquarian with his pick, must account for him. This gigantic shadow falls across every study table; this immense personality stands at the crucible in every laboratory.

There are two ways of reaching the top of Mount Washington. You may start from Crawford's Notch; mile after mile you may struggle over rock and yawning chasm, until tired and torn, you reach at last the rest and outlook at the summit. Or you may take the little car at Fabyan's, and, without effort or risk, in a very short time you may be looking down upon the far-away world. So there are men who are eagerly seeking the great explanation of the world's good. They look for it in science; they interrogate the long shelves of the world's libraries; they grope for footprints in the fields and mountains; they listen with strained ears for voices in the shout of the thunder or the song of the jubilant sea. After infinite struggle and disappointment they find a dim shadow, a "power that makes for righteousness," a "promise and potency of all terrestrial life." And at once they are ready to say, "These be thy gods, O Israel, which have brought thee up out of the beginnings and the ignoble."

But there is a shorter route to the mountain summit, a surer way to the explanation. In the chapters that follow we have sought to consider some of the problems of the modern world, and have noted the solution as suggested by theorists or as wrought out by the slow process of time. Everywhere have we found Him of whom Moses and the prophets did write. "Whatsoever things are true, whatsoever things are honest, whatsoever things are just, whatsoever things are pure, whatsoever things are lovely, whatsoever things are of good report," we may look for their spring and inspiration in Bethlehem. "If there be any virtue, and if there be any praise," it is of Jesus Christ. His friends have been the friends of reform; his followers have given the upward look to history. Take any point of departure, go in any direction, pass through the ranks of the world's heroes, or the world's scholars, or the world's philanthropists—those who have enlarged life, who have given a diviner meaning to progress and a sweeter meaning to service—and, sooner or later, you come face to face with the living, loving Christ. He is not only the Author of our faith, but the Author of our civilization. He not only saves us from sin and littleness and atrophy, but he saves us to the largest, fullest life; not only in the Old Testament sense of elimination, but in the New Testament sense of reconstruction and evolution.

> "And so the Word had breath and wrought
>   With human hands the creed of creeds
>   In loveliness of perfect deeds,
> More strong than all poetic thought;
>
> "Which he may read that binds the sheaf,
>   Or builds the house, or digs the grave,
>   And those wild eyes that watch the wave
> In roaring round the coral reef,"

I

THE SURVIVAL OF THE FITTEST

Back to Bethlehem

I

The Survival of the Fittest

THE first prophecy of the Old Testament is a declaration of war. It is a message from the Commander in Chief that his flag will soon be afield. According to the traditional setting, it was spoken amid the kind foliage of a virgin world. It was heard by a man and a woman whose range was narrow and whose ideas were primitive, but it contains the marching orders of the ages. It maps out the campaigns of all the future. The world was to be a scene of struggle. This is the burden of this weird old-time tocsin. Life had been ideal. The sun had risen upon the Golden Age. There was no serpent Ladon in the Garden of the Hesperides. The three maidens from Jötunheim who brought dissension and ruin had not yet entered Asgard, the sunny land "midway between the regions of frost and ice."

But a change was coming. There was to be a mustering of forces, and the next move in the history of the race was to be a skirmish for position. The race, or what there was of it, had been a child. It had thought as a child, and understood as a child, but the prohibition of the tree of knowledge of good and evil meant that it was on the threshold of manhood and must henceforth live the life of a man. The story of Eden is the story of a man, the story of men. Hegel claims that "the Fall is the eternal Mythus of Man—in fact, the very transition by which he becomes Man"; first the innocence and tranquillity of instinct, then the self-consciousness and unrest of reason. The man and the woman dressed and kept the garden, and gave names to the beasts of the field; they were naked and unashamed. But the new sensations of curiosity and desire destroyed the animal content. It was the harmony of childhood breaking up in the discords of manhood. It was the knowledge of good and evil by which man became as God. This is the story of life. Donatello, the frolicsome spirit who gambols through the earlier chapters of the Marble Faun, comes one day into contact with matters of awful moment. Prompted by the glance of a strong-willed woman, he takes the life of a human being. Says Hawthorne, "His form had dilated. It had kindled him into a man. The simple and joyous creature whom he had hitherto known was now gone forever." In one supreme moment he had crossed the bar at the mouth of the harbor and had been smitten by the sea blast. He had become a man and had entered upon man's inheritance of struggle and extremity. He had eaten of the forbidden fruit and had been driven forth from the paradise of instinct and childish simplicity. The world was all before him, but it was a world in which henceforth his bread was to be eaten by the sweat of his brow. This same lesson is learned by Parsifal in the garden of temptation where the kiss of Kundry is the fruit from the tree of knowledge. Bonaventura, shy, selfish, impulsive, passionate, delivers his rival to the conscript officers, and then goes into travail. His "ora-a-a" of exultation is followed by bitter days and sleepless nights, out of which comes a beautiful unselfishness which makes his life and character an inspiration and an ideal. So over and over again is told in real life and in romance the splendid old

story of the world's beginning—how out of
the knowledge of good and evil is born soul-
consciousness, the arrival of selfhood; yea, the
death of innocence, threatened by the powers
of good; and the god-knowledge of right and
wrong promised by the powers of evil, who
told a mighty truth in the midst of a mighty
lie.

Even if we are not ready to accept all
that Evolution may seek to teach us, at the
same time we are not deaf to all of its data.
It depends largely upon the spirit and phraseology of the teacher. Mr. Charles Darwin
came upon the platform with his Descent of
Man, and there was a gathering of the clans
and the cry of "no quarter" was heard all
along the line. There was an implied reflection upon the race in the very title of the book.
There was a suggestion of down-grade, and
the treatise was prejudged and its conclusions
outlawed before the pages were dry. We are
more tolerant with Henry Drummond. He
may bring us along the same path. He may
look for our beginnings in the same "her-
maphrodite ascidian." But he has been shrewd
enough to call the process of change The
Ascent of Man, and lo, we are ready to place
his book in our liturgy and canonize its au-

thor. There is nothing repulsive nor humiliating in the thought that our bodies are the result of growth; that the forms we possess, the dignity and grace of our physical humanity, are the climax of ages of planning and of experiment and of development; that even as the human embryo passes through the forms of the lower animals, borrowing from each some characteristic and carrying it on to the next stage, until in the end it has become a combination of all the best things below it; so the race has struggled on and up by a long and tedious way, until at last the human body is a microcosm, a sodality of all created excellence, a part of all it has met and of all it has been as it journeyed toward the mountain top. All this we leave with the scientist, assured of our mental tranquillity however the matter is settled.

But it is at this stage that the struggle is transferred to a new plane and new factors are to be considered. The body has come into its kingdom. It has reached the mountain peak. But there are peaks beyond peaks. The summit of the physical is only the base of the spiritual. No sooner has the body reached its perihelion than a new agent appears, a new struggle begins, a new Richmond is in the field.

The steed of instinct which has ranged at will is to have a strong rider. The battle royal is transferred from the realm of matter to the realm of spirit. The field of operations has been objective, now it is to become subjective. The assault and schism have been from influences without, now these are to come from influences within. We are complete animals. The beasts that roam the woods or browze in the fields or dig in the earth are kindred of the flesh with the animal we call man, even though he has learned to dress and undress himself and eat his food when cooked. If we were only animal we would have a much easier time of it. There is perfect content for those beings only who are either purely animal or purely spiritual. Only at the summit and at the base of creation is there peace. Take away all the animal from man and his life would become tranquil, the tranquillity of the lake at the mountain summit, above the dust of the lowlands and the tides of the sea. Take away all the spiritual from man and he will become tranquil, the tranquillity of the stagnant pool in the mountain cavern shielded from the gleam and stir of the day. But so long as these two warring elements meet in the same personality, so long will there be struggle and travail until one or the other has surrendered and wears its rival's chains and does its rival's bidding.

There is a right and there is a wrong always encamped over against it, sending out its Goliath armed with coat of mail and thundering his defiance. There is a nobler nature in man, "the hate of hate, the scorn of scorn, the love of love"; a something that finds God and seeks to be like him. It is this which has made heroes. It has founded religions. It has sung psalms at the stake. It came from heaven and it knows the way back, and its face is turned in that direction. But it is not a cleared path in which it treads. The way lies through the enemy's country. There is stratagem, and ambush, and open battle. Every inch of the road must be contested. Dr. Jekyll always has his Edward Hyde; Cicero has his Cataline; William the Silent his Count Egmont; even Jesus had a Judas making a part of his environment and complicating the problem of life. This is the experience of the individual. The best resolutions are broken; the noblest impulses are strangled; the grandest victory over wrong may in the next moment be converted into a defeat. This is the experience of the race. The literature of all peoples has been full of battle sounds. It has voiced the agony of the soul in the grip of a giant. In the oldest of the Vedas, written on the tablelands of Asia while Moses was keeping the flocks of Midian, we read:

"O hear this my calling, Varuna, be gracious now,
  Longing for help I have called upon thee."

"Now, now thou art moist clay," writes Flaccus in the gray dawn before the day of Bethlehem, "thou must be shaped by the glowing wheel." Earlier still Noah toils for one hundred and twenty years on the ark, putting God into every stroke of the hammer; building a refuge for himself and for his family from the deluge and from depravity. But the spirit of drunkenness went with him from the ark, and one of the sons who had dwelt with him in the consecrated vessel betrayed him with mocking and scorn. Simeon the Stylite spent thirty awful years on the top of a great column, an undressed sheepskin on his back, a grazing iron collar about his neck. Yet there was no escape from the strife.

"I hardly with slow steps,
With slow faint steps and much exceeding pain,
Have scrambled past those pits of fire that still
Sing in my ears."

It is a heart struggle, a battle in the deeps and dark of the human soul, and every man carries about with him the battle ground.

Moreover, we can never go back to the lower ranges. Once having reached the level of the spirit we can never return to the purely carnal. We are born on the up-grade. To reverse the machinery would violate the instincts of our nature and clash with the eternal processes of life. Reversion to type may bestialize the humanity that is within us, but it can never destroy the fact that we are human, nor strangle all our human longings. There is no hope for us in the lowlands whence we have come, so the ambition of the profoundest faiths has been to seek quiet at the summit. Buddhism, the reaction against a degenerate Brahmanism, may be summed up in its four "Sublime Verities": 1. Existence is only pain and sorrow. 2. The cause of pain and sorrow is desire. 3. In Nirvana all pain and sorrow cease. 4. The way to attain Nirvana is by self-discipline, ending in the oblivion of self-consciousness. This Nirvana is dangerously like annihilation. Struggle and turmoil in life, this struggle arising from the clash between the animal and the spiritual; there is no help even in the grave; the spirit that has not conquered its environment, that is not completely master, enters at death into another existence and the struggle is renewed; there is but one escape, but one refuge; when all desires are destroyed, when the soul walks alone, stripped, hypnotic, in a barren world, then the Arahat has attained Nirvana, and living or dead he is at peace.

So taught the stoics of Greek philosophy. They sought *apatheia,* a state of mind in which the passions are extinguished by the ascendency of reason. This is the only true wisdom: the destruction of emotion, the rooting out of affection, the subordination of every instinct and impulse, the power to endure. "When you kiss your little child or wife think, 'I kiss a mortal,' and so you shall not be troubled when they die," is the best that Epictetus can offer. The promise of the Serpent Bruiser had not reached the ears of Buddha. The porches of Athens were separated by measureless distances from the green groves of Eden. They looked and there was none to help, they wondered that there was none to uphold.

The first prophecy of the Bible is not only a declaration of war, it is also a pæan of victory. The right will triumph by and by. It may be a long time on the road, but it is coming. There may be whirlpools and deep eddies in the river that seem to be creeping upstream, but the great waters have heard the call of the sea, and they are moving steadily seaward. It was a dark day in Eden when sin first became a factor in human life and history. The world plan seemed to have failed. Before that fateful hour God's favorite word had been "bless." And God blessed the living creatures, and bade them multiply and fill the waters in the seas; and God blessed the man and the woman, and bade them multiply and replenish the earth and subdue it; and God blessed the seventh day and sanctified it, because in it he had rested from all his work. This had been the keynote of the song of creation. But now God begins to speak of things as "cursed." The earth had been man's enthusiastic ally, now it was to be his unwilling servant doing his bidding only under the lash. The tree of life had been in the midst of the garden and within easy reach; now only he that overcometh is to eat of this tree; and the overcoming is the struggle by which we are to reach the goal of human endeavor, the conquest of self, the triumph of right.

But the Deliverer and the deliverance are

coming. This is the message that comes to us from these days of the world's kindergarten. The power of evil is to be broken, the right is to prevail, the woman who first yielded to evil is to have a large share of the final triumph.

This triumph of right is not in the nature of things. The race is not to grow into perfection. Evolution may produce the physical man, but it cannot perfect him. The Ten Commandments are not written on the tables of natural law. The Sermon on the Mount is not the last chapter of the book of material development. The ladder up which we have climbed lacks the highest round, and this must elsewhere be found. If any man would be ready to magnify the natural process and to be satisfied with it, that man was Mr. Huxley. Yet he said in his Romanes lecture, "Let us understand once for all that the ethical progress of society depends not on imitating the cosmic process, but in combating it." Man has come to his high estate by the "cosmic process," that is, by the successful exercise of qualities which he shares with the ape and the tiger. "Now," says Mr. Huxley, "he would be only too pleased to see the ape and the tiger die." Traits which mean success in a savage state may become criminal in higher civilization. The struggle for life which guarantees the safety and the development of the animal, when translated into the struggle for a seat in a crowded car or the struggle for position in public life, marks the boor or the ward politician.

This victory of the race is not to be achieved in the material world. Cotton looms and smokeless powder do not conquer sin. Physical science can never redeem the soul. It can do almost everything else. It is the servant of man, the friend of the race, the conqueror of nature. It has added to the years of human life. In the sixteenth century the length of a generation in Switzerland was twenty-one years; in the twentieth century it is forty years. The discovery of quinine has added two years to the expectation of life. In the seventeenth century the British government announced that ten thousand of each sex died under the age of twenty-eight, against six thousand who died at the same age one century later. Science has broadened our world, opened the door for travel and discovery, and given us leisure for these pursuits by doing our work for us. It has provided us with weapons so that we can travel with safety, and with machinery by which we can travel with speed. This earth which was once the supreme object of our knowledge is now only one of a sisterhood of worlds; the skies have opened to us and we are citizens of a universe. The Saracens gave us the art of making paper, and the Venetians brought us printing blocks from China. Then Coster, or Gutenberg, or Faust, or Schöffer, as the case may be, made his movable type, and then, down went the despotisms and ignorance of the Middle Ages. The mariner's compass gave America to the world; the chronometer made the long trackless voyage safe.

In all this do we see the hand of science. But the way of salvation is not there. The principalities, the powers, the world rulers of this darkness are not to be conquered by modern cannon. The spiritual hosts of wickedness in heavenly places are not to be exorcised by the whistle of the factory or the fog horn of the ships. The perfect man is not the result of any new chemical formula nor the outcome of any new medical school. Sin is just as treacherous, and disobedience to God is just as easy and just as fatal, as it was when our fathers wore their undressed wolfskins in Britain, or wandered homeless and kingless through the vast forests of Germany.

But may there not be other enterprises of the brain to which we may look for help? This intellect, the crowning glory of the race, may it not be the Moses to lead the race to spiritual freedom? If so, then is our deliverance close at hand, for this is veritably the age of reason. If so, this will simplify the process. Our salvation will then be a native product. We will save ourselves. Out of our own resources will the strong web be spun that is to lift us over the abysses. The good thing will then come out of Nazareth, and will be in every sense a Nazarene. The public school will then not only drive away ignorance, but it will conquer sin. The binomial theorem, the rule of three, will not merely discipline the brain, but they will purify the heart. Here is a glimpse of Utopia, a return of the Golden Age—Pericles without Aspasia, Calvin without Servetus, Cromwell without Drogheda; supremacy of intellect without improbity; supremacy of faith without fanaticism; an alliance of the mental and the spiritual that would hasten the millennium.

But intellect is selfish. It is not interested in the general good. Its inventions are patented, its books are copyrighted. It does not throw aside the stage coach for the express to save time for the public, but to increase the company's receipts. It applies the best machinery and the best chemistry to wheat growing not that the price of wheat be cheapened and the poor be fed, but that the cost of producing be reduced; even controlling the output and creating a panic so that the price may be kept at paying figures. And what does intellect care for the race as such? To be sure, literature is full of sublime passages. Unselfishness, heroism, the loftiest devotion to principle are taught in poetry and prose; but these sentiments come not from the brain alone. They are the utterances of the heart. The brain says so often with Hobbes, "Why are friendships good things? Because they are useful. Why do we pity another? Because we imagine a similar misfortune may happen to us." Human salvation was not to be wrought out by the intellect. Edgar Allan Poe gave the world a tremendous sermon when he wrote The Raven. With inspired genius he left the bird of ill omen perched upon Pallas, the goddess of wisdom. Despair sometimes hovers over knowledge, never over faith. There was no cross of the Crucified in that doomed spirit-haunted chamber. The Raven would not have stayed if there had been. And from all the crossless, Christless chambers of the human soul, shelved with knowledge and draped with the purple silken curtains of pride, there has ever gone up the same hopeless dirge:

"And the Raven, never flitting, still is sitting, still is sitting
On the pallid bust of Pallas, just above my chamber door;
And his eyes have all the seeming of a demon's that is dreaming,
And the lamplight o'er him streaming throws his shadow on the floor;
And my soul from out that shadow that lies floating on the floor
        Shall be lifted—nevermore!"

It is the Seed of the woman who is to bruise the serpent's head. The promise of Bethlehem is the promise of power. The coming of the Christ is to be the coming of the Conqueror. He went to the mountain top with the tempter and the glory of the world was offered him. He refused, because he asked no favors of his enemies. The ambitious mother asked him that her sons might sit the one on the right, the other on the left, when he occupied his throne. He was then on his way to the thorn crown and the sealed sepulcher. But he answered as though there would be such positions as the woman coveted and that they would be worth occupying. He was pinioned to the cross; the powers of the church and the state were combined against him, and he was certainly dying. Yet when the man dying with him prayed, "Lord, remember me when thou comest in thy kingdom," he replied, "This day shalt thou be with me in paradise," as if he were still master of the situation and only Lord of paradise. His dead body lay all night long and all day, and through another night, in the sealed sepulcher, and when in the early dawn the angels hurried from the skies to roll away the stone they found the helpless guards prostrate upon the earth, an empty tomb, an Easter morning breaking gloriously over the hills, and a world already beginning to quiver with the consciousness of his presence and the awful sense of his supreme power.

It is the triumph of a new kind of life which he came to bring, and to bring more abundantly. And because he lives this new victorious life we are to live it also. We are to tread down not only the evil in our own life, but the evil in the world life. The serpent of oppression and injustice and greed must be crushed, and we in Christ are to do it. It is the survival of the fittest; the higher life in conflict with the lower and conquering it. The author of Christ in Modern Life says, "That man is able to live the morality of Christ is a modern idea." And yet it is contained in the first prophecy. It is the newest orthodoxy and it is part of the very oldest faith. "Whatsoever is born of God overcometh the world;" and the world means anything whereby our brother stumbleth or is offended or is made weak. And the world may be found in the marts of trade, in the whirl of society, or within the chambers of the heart.

II
ENVIRONMENT

II

Environment

THE "Great Unknown" of the schools strikes a high key in the opening of Isa. 63. Whatever the verdict of the historic critics as to the time and authorship of these words, the literary critics have no controversy as to their sublimity. The vision of the blood-stained conqueror coming from Edom, "marching in the greatness of his strength," is inspiring whether we view it as the work of Isaiah the Benjamite, looking out upon the tremblings of Judah and projecting himself by the power of his seership into the days of the Babylonian captivity; or the work of the Deutero-Isaiah of the exile, whose earnest purpose was to save the people from despair, and who has given us thus anonymously the most magnificent passages of the revealed will of God. Whether written years before the events described, or in the midst of those events, the words are large words. They touch far horizons. They foreshadow conditions and methods of our modern life. The warrior from

Edom is an important factor in the solution of present-day religious problems. He is a contemporary.

The critical objection that this and the following chapters are too clearly prophetic, and that they must therefore be assigned to a later date, is unfounded, since they as certainly foreshadow the conditions and successes of the present as they do the deliverance of Israel from Babylon and Edom. We are fulfilling in our churches and in our evangelizing plans the predictions of this chapter. Here is the plan of campaign. The seer looks down the long and winding gorges that lead up to Jerusalem from the Jordan. Suddenly a strange figure appears. It has come from the mountains that lie beyond. It has crossed the river and is moving majestically up the heights of Judea. There are marks of conflict. There is the air of victory. The champion of Israel has been in Edom and has won his greatest triumphs there.

It is useless to repeat here the venerable statement that Edom, the hereditary foe of Israel, typifies the evil of the world. Phillips Brooks has woven this thought with threads of light in his own inimitable way, and everyone who has handled this subject since has

ENVIRONMENT

but copied his pattern. The prophecy is a foreshadowing of the victory of Christ, a victory that is rewon every century and that is written out in the history of the Christian church. Edom had been more malevolent even than Chaldea. These sons of Esau were fiercer in their enmity toward Israel than the sons of strangers. In the time of their hegira the Israelites were refused permission to pass through their land though they promised to turn neither to the right nor to the left, and even to pay for the water they drank.[1] In the day of the overthrow of Jerusalem these recreant sons of Abraham had cried out, "Rase it, rase it even to the foundations thereof."[2] They had "spoken proudly in the day of distress, and rejoiced proudly over the children of Judah in the day of their destruction."[3] They had even lain in ambush on the "crossways" to Egypt to cut off those that did escape and to deliver them into the hands of the Chaldeans.

Into the very stronghold of this bitter foe the Conqueror had gone. He did not wait invasion. He was so strong and so self-confident and so insistent that he was ready to take the initiative. It is comparatively easy

[1] Num. 20. 14, 21.   [2] Psa. 137. 7.   [3] Obad. 12.

to defend. The Alps are better than armies for Switzerland. The English Channel is the guardian and the guarantee of English homes. That little strip of silver sea has marked the limit of oppression and serfdom. On the oceanward side England has sat and built her ships and trained her sons and nursed her virtues, and there is nothing on the landward side that has dared to cross with hostile intent. It took three Federal soldiers four years to conquer one Confederate. Not that the latter was a better soldier, but he was at home, and the former were invaders. De Block, the Russian who suggested The Hague Tribunal to the Czar, holds that with our modern weapons one man in defense is equal to ten men on the offensive. But said this majestic warrior:

"I looked and there was none to help;
Therefore mine own arm brought salvation to me,
And my fury it upheld me."

Over into Edom he crossed. He scaled the heights of Teman. Like a lion from the thickets of Jordan he sprang upon the flocks amid the rock pastures of the Negeb. He spread out his wings like an eagle over Bozrah. It was more than good triumphant; it was good intrusive, good aggressive, good intolerant. It is David who invades the territory of the giant with a challenge; it is the reform that does not wait for attack.

These are modern religious tactics. The work of the church is not defensive but offensive. It has had enough of apologetics that were apologies; it wants a stiff course of polemics as a tonic. It fails if it wait for doors to open. The doors are to be opened from without, and the true faith does not long wait on the threshold. A church that is only conservative, that expends its energies in merely holding its own, does not deserve to have any own to hold; it deserves to die, it is dying. This is the contention of Max Müller. He claims that the nonmissionary faiths are dead faiths. The religion of the Mazdeans, for instance, is narrow and exclusive. It seeks no converts, it makes no invasions, and it has been reduced in the last three centuries to a mere fraction of its ancient strength. Only about one hundred thousand souls remain of the great hosts that once burned the Bahram fire and worshiped Ahuramazda. These refuse to admit to their communion any convert not of pure Parsee blood, and Zoroastrianism, as it is popularly called, is doomed.

Here is the hope and the salvation of Christianity. Its blood is kept fresh by constant infusion. It has always been a missionary faith. The tongues as of fire that came at Pentecost, and that endowed the disciples with speech intelligible to Parthians and Medes and devout men out of every nation, were a prophecy and a preparation. Here was the physical organ typical of this new enterprise—the tongue; here was a message all could understand; these were the accredited messengers who would soon be on the road. The divine command is, "Go into all the world;" the divine promise is, "I am with you alway;" the divine purpose is that this witnessing, begun at Jerusalem, should extend to the uttermost parts of the earth.

The apostles were missionaries. The book of Acts is a record of missionary enterprise and effort. Its churches are mission stations and its chapters are swift reports from the field. By the end of the first century there were two hundred thousand members of the Christian faith. At the end of the third century five per cent of the Roman empire had been reached and had yielded. Then, when the politician Constantine by legal edict made Christianity the state religion, the irrepressible faith turned its eyes outward to look for other worlds to conquer. The Mediterranean was girdled by the cross, but beyond the sweep of the Roman road and beyond the gleam of the Roman eagle there were barbarism and ignorance. The Arian scholar Ulfilas crossed the Danube with a new alphabet which told the old sweet story to the Goths. Frumentius, the "Father of Peace," went south and the historic Abyssinian church began its checkered career of a thousand years.

Honoratus founded a missionary training institute and sent evangelists to capture the Rhone valley, the land of olives and sunshine. Christopher Columbus sailed from Palos as a missionary. In the prologue to his journal, which he intended for the inspection of the Spanish sovereigns, he speaks of the Grand Khan of India who had sent to Rome for instructors in the true faith; and because this request had not been granted, "so many people were lost, believing in idolatries and imbibing doctrines of perdition." He then continues: "Therefore your Highnesses as Catholic Christians and princes, lovers and promoters of the holy Christian faith and enemies of the sect of Mohammed and of all idolatries and heresies, determined to send me, Christopher Columbus, to the said parts of India to see the said princes and the people and lands, and discover the nature and disposition of them all, and the means to be taken for the conversion of them to our holy faith." America was discovered by a missionary on his way to save the world.

Francis Xavier, Matthew Ricci, Las Casas, are names that flame out like beacon fires amid the shadows of the Middle Ages. The parting gift of Sir Walter Raleigh to the colonists of Virginia was one hundred pounds for the propagation of the Christian religion in America. Side by side with ideas of colonization were ideas of evangelization. The first convert in America was baptized August 13, 1587; the first child of European parents was born August 18 of the same year. The new continent was thus given by ceremonial rite to Christianity five days before the first infant opened its eyes amid the unconquered forest and became the forerunner of the new race that soon would dominate the land.

The sporadic attempts mentioned above were but prophecies. A new programme of missions has been published. Within the past century Christianity has adopted the world. Hitherto the church has busily cultivated its own vineyard. Its reforms have been intramural; its warfare has been defensive. Here and there, as already noted, straggling parties have gone out and a desultory guerrilla style of tactics has prevailed. But its Luthers and Bezas and Knoxes have needed all their strength to keep pure the faith once delivered to the fathers. To-day, however, we suspect a Christian spirit which is not at the same time a missionary spirit. We have no use for a faith that does not realize the world, and that is not ready to put its arms around the whole world. The race has broken with the cults that were localized by custom or tradition. The Nile gods, the Olympian muster roll, these recipients of a primal faith have been left lonely and forgotten in their ancient haunts. They were vital and alert on their native heath, but the world does not any longer crouch by the banks of the Egyptian river nor catch a glimpse of Olympus from its housetops. It is a larger world than it used to be.

The old creeds that limited the divine grace and election, the self-centered cult of Israel, the huge egoism of the Romanist, the pathetic inexorable syllogisms of Calvin—all these have beaten themselves out upon a persistent and a growing individualism; and more and more has it come home to man that the only bounds to the divine purpose of redemption are the bounds we ourselves set. Nothing less than a cosmopolitan offer of salvation will satisfy the Christian intelligence of the day. We have revised our spiritual geographies until they correspond with the "whole world" of the apostolic commission. Our missionary maps are on the Mercator's projection, and the great round globe may be seen at a glance. The Conqueror has crossed into Edom. The church is strong enough because Christlike enough to take the initiative—not spasmodically, nor in desultory sorties; the constructor has gone out with the sappers and miners, and wherever the church has conquered it has colonized.

There is marked improvement in the attitude of the church in another particular. It does not wait for the people to come to it; it goes to the people. The Great Supper of the parable has taken upon itself some new and striking developments. The servants have been sent to say to them that were bidden, "Come, for all things are now ready;" and these have made their excuses. Now out into the streets and lanes of the city, the highways and hedges of the country, the servants are gone, not so much to compel the people to come to the feast as to carry the feast to the people. This is current. The modern workman carries his tools to the work. The sawmill is placed in the midst of the virgin forest, the wheat is made ready for the market in the field, the miner carries his steam or hydraulic drill into the narrowest passages of the mine.

Going into Edom, this is the new plan of campaign. Our downtown churches no longer

> "fold their tents, like the Arabs,
> And as silently steal away."

They are modifying their plans and adjusting their plants to meet the new conditions. Our new enterprises in unpropitious or undeveloped soil are no longer "missions." They are "branches," and they have behind them the vital resources of the great body that planted them. They are expected to grow into independent individual members of the organization for which they stand. The great cathedrals of Europe are lineal descendants of the temple at Jerusalem—one degree removed from the temple, it is true, since they represent an oligarchy instead of a monarchy. There is still, however, the idea of exclusion and of caste. The people must still make their pilgrimages to a Mecca or a Zion. Gerizim and Moriah are still rival centers of religious enthusiasm and power. But the later churches that Christianity has built as the swift expedients to meet a local need have been a concession to growing democracy. Like the cities of refuge they have been brought within the sphere of the people and placed within easy reach and convenience. Christianity has gone out among the people, and the churches have followed Christianity.

We do not want any cathedrals in America. The spirit that localizes Christianity is the spirit of mediævalism. The splendid old piles that have come down to us from the past are eloquent monuments of dead ideals. They remind us of the day when the people existed for the church and not the church for the people. They do not so much represent the religion as the political ethics of the past, for the church was then but another name for the state, and both held οἱ πολλοί in contempt.

The Institutional church is an army division thrown out into the enemy's country and garrisoned there. It is a phase of religious expansion. It is an invasion of Edom. The day nurseries and kindergartens are teaching the language of Canaan in the schools of the Edomites, making it the speech of court and market place. The free dispensaries, the deaconesses, the Mercy and Help Departments are the Red Cross contingents of the invading army, and Edom has not seen the like of this before.

"A poor man saved by thee shall make thee rich;
A sick man helped by thee shall make thee strong.
Thou shalt be served thyself by every sense
Of service which thou renderest."

We hear a great deal about environment. This is the ghost of Banquo at many of our feasts, and it has rather a confirmed and confident habit of shaking its gory locks at us whenever we suggest improvement or essay reform. "Heredity and environment," says a modern high priest of religious sociology, "are the master influences of the world. They have made us what we are." Over the former, of course, we have no control as it may affect our life. The influence of the latter is therefore to be considered, and this influence is manifest in animate and inanimate creation, and is one of the most intricate problems in the question of reform. The root of monkshood, from which is extracted an extremely poisonous alkaloid when grown in its native soil, becomes harmless when transplanted to the frozen North. The splendid oak of our American forests loses its dignity and takes a plebeian place in South Africa. The spicy sassafras of this continent loses its spice in Europe. The intoxicating hemp of India lacks its festive qualities when grown in sedate England. The oyster, inert and unresponsive as we are pleased to believe it, if taken from the waters of the Atlantic and dropped into the Mediterranean begins to refashion its garments in the style of its new associates. It learns to conform to the world in which it lives; it does as Rome does.

This power of environment is everywhere at work. It affects the child in the cradle, the boy on the playground, the whole life from beginning to end. It is the mold in which the character is cast, the background against which and on account of which the chameleon takes its color. All this is claimed, and the amount of truth in the claim is startling. A man depends very much upon the company he keeps for the good or bad elements in his life. This was a Sunday school truism before it became a scientific formula. His occupation will leave its imprint upon his face or in his mental methods. Two children of the same parentage, placed under radically different home treatment, will develop radically different traits. The ideas and ideals of the home give shape and tendency to the life. We do not look in the slums for the refinements of the closely guarded family circle where only that which is pure is seen and heard.

Here, then, is the scheme of modern fatalism; born well—placed well—all well. But let there be a bar sinister in the crest, a dash of sediment in the blood; let the conditions of life be adverse, the soul born on the downgrade, and as fixed as the stars in their courses, so certain will be the life wreck and the soul ruin of the doomed victim. There is no help in Edom for the Edomite. But the Conqueror has crossed the river and is face to face with conditions on the farther side. The modern Christ goes within the sweep of the maelstrom of environment and plucks the doomed wretch out of the swirl of ruin. The modern messenger of Christ lives on the same street with those who need him most. The city missionary, the Salvation Army, the rescue worker not only resist in themselves the power of environment, but they break that power over others.

Here Christianity meets a new philosophy of life. Science has said that a man is what he sees and absorbs every day. Now, declares this philosophy, change his surroundings and you will change the man. Remodel the tenement house, ventilate the workshop, regulate the hours and conditions of labor, and you redeem the race. Give the man a bathtub and a bookshelf and a flowerpot, and you give him a new ideal and a new inspiration. This is our gospel of humanity. The salvation of the world is to be effected by social reform, by the physical and domestic elevation of the submerged tenth. The "new revival" is creating quite a stir; and this is the scheme: "There was a day when a preacher could appeal to his hearer and awaken his heart to praise because God had saved him while thousands had been left to perish, but to-day the hearer would firmly suspend his praise for his own salvation till he knew what was going to become of other people. No longer does a man think that the great effort of life should be, as the Romans say, 'to make his own soul,' but rather that it should be to help his brethren both in soul and body. A sermon on the hell beyond the grave would be heard with indifference; a sermon on the hell in the east end of cities will lay hold on every man's mind. The sense is creeping over the community that socially and physically we stand together, and religion cannot remain a water-tight compartment of spiritual selfishness. With such a tide running like a mill race and such a wind blowing like a gale upon one's face, have we not reason to expect that the message of the next revival will be social righteousness, and its effect the redemption of the national life?"[1]

There is much of truth in this, but not all the truth. The church has always been engaged in social service, and has always stood for social reform. But the church that neglects the individual, that makes its first and main appeal to the improvement of economic conditions, is little better than a social club. First convert the man, and then he will proceed to change his environment. Make him dissatisfied with Edom and he will modify Edom. Send him home some night with a clean heart and a new love, and he will see that the wretched hovel in which he has housed his wife and children—bare and cold and cheerless—is not home; that the wan, hopeless woman and the hollow-eyed little

[1] The Rev. John Watson: The New Revival.

ones who meet him there have not had their share of life, and that he is to blame for it. The prodigal started back to his father when his environment was at its worst. Solomon made a dismal failure of his life in spite of the most favorable conditions. The environment of Abraham Lincoln may easily be duplicated in the far West; and out of such conditions has come a large harvest of rawboned, overgrown rustics, but there has been only one Lincoln. The quiet hills about Stratford, the thatched cottages, the gently flowing Avon, explain nothing of the mastership of Shakespeare,

> "Who walked in every path of human life,
> Felt every passion."

The pond lily can grow from the foulest quagmire. The Bowery may not be a promising field, but it is not a hopeless one. Much depends upon what is planted there and who plants it. The soul that finds its affinity in such surroundings will absorb the contagion and will ultimately add to the corruption. But the soul that repudiates the evil, that finds its correspondence with the good only, such a soul will keep itself clean in spite of the cesspool in which it grows. "Whosoever is born of God doth not commit sin, for his seed remaineth in him." The seed planted takes from the soil that for which it has affinity. The seed of wheat absorbs starch, the maple searches and finds that which can be converted into sugar; the melon seed drinks water even in the dry places. So the seed of God in the human heart draws to itself that which is high and noble, and out of the eater comes forth meat and out of the strong comes forth sweetness, even as Samson gathered golden honey from the sun-dried skeleton of the Syrian lion.

Let the Christ Conqueror go into the slums and he will prevail against the slums. Let him become the environment of the soul and it may laugh at all other environment. Let a man be able to say, "In him I live, and move, and have my being," and it matters little where else he may live. In his Comus Milton writes:

> "Some say no evil thing that walks by night
> In fog or fire, by lake or moorish fen,
> Blue meager hag or stubborn unlaid ghost
> That breaks his magic chains at curfew time,
> No goblin or swart faery of the mine,
> Hath hurtful power o'er true virginity."

So let the soul be fixed in its fidelity to God and it is proof against the impulse of inherited appetite, the appeal of contiguous allurement, or the inertia of habitual assent. It is superior to its world environment. It has found for itself a new correspondence, and "neither death, nor life, nor angels, nor principalities, nor powers, nor things present, nor things to come, nor height, nor depth, nor any other creature," can ever separate it from its newer choice or drag it back into a hopeless Edom.

III
THE UNITY OF THE RACE

III

The Unity of the Race

EVEN in America we are beginning to be interested in "endless genealogies which minister questions." There are coats of arms on our parlor walls and armorial bearings on the panels of our landaus. Some of us are content to be known as Sons, or Daughters, of the Revolution; others file their claim to distinction because of hypothetical family connection with a conjectural Mayflower passenger list. Still others trace their lineage back to some blustering Dick Turpin of the rare old days when highway robbery meant knighthood instead of Newgate. But there is always a point beyond which these claims cannot go. Sooner or later the clew is lost. The roots of the great family tree, like all well-behaved roots, are out of sight.

There is, to be sure, a vague general notion prevalent among proper-minded people that the lines of ancestry converge in Adam; but these lines have never been explored fully, and even the notion itself does not lack contradition. The fact is that as we move back toward the beginning we find a manifest disinclination to accept a single beginning. The idea of race unity can scarcely be called intuitive. There was no brotherhood of man among the primitive men. The native traditions of the early peoples usually dealt with the origin of their own clan, and invariably claimed for themselves priority of creation, or superiority of endowment. Seven generations of heavenly deities were followed by five generations of earthly deities, and then came the mortal sovereigns, according to Japanese myth. Menes, the founder of Memphis, was the first mortal ruler of the Egyptians. Before him had been eight gods; back of these a series of twelve greater gods, then Osiris, then Typhon, then in the remotest past Horus; and from this patrician and exclusive beginning came the people of the Nile valley. Four races of mankind were recognized here—the red, the yellow, the black, and the white. Red was the sacred, the aristocratic color; and so the Egyptians have painted themselves on their monuments. The Athenians called themselves *Autochthones,* or those who have sprung from the soil; all others were *Barbaroi,* foreigners. The Chinese stoutly keep up this distinction and its resultant comfortable self-esteem, and are slow to readjust their ethnological tables. And even our boys and girls were taught until a recent date to divide the race into enlightened, civilized, half-civilized, and barbarous; the authors of this tabulation always claiming reserved seats in the first section.

The further back we go the more hopelessly divided seems the race according to its own traditions. As we approach the source of the stream there is an insistent suggestion of divers sources. Even Israel, with its ancient documents concerning Eden and the confusion of tongues, did not appreciate race unity. Her prophets might take a theologic, or let us say an academic, interest in Chaldea and Tyre, but not one of them could be found willing to undertake a mission to Nineveh. The Christian religion, however, or at any rate its earlier exponents, committed themselves to a blood relationship. Paul of Tarsus stood among the proud *Autochthones* in the shadow of the Acropolis, and declared that God "made of one (blood) every nation of men for to dwell on all the face of the earth." The courtly audience on Mars' Hill dismissed this social reformer with unimpeachable suavity and well-bred phrases, but he was dismissed none the less. This was not the spirit of the *Akademeia* and the *Stoa*. This dictum of the apostle to the Gentiles has been regarded as decisive, and the basis of this new ethnology now to be championed by Christianity is the tenth chapter of Genesis. This was believed to settle all questions as to origin or unity. Here is a table of "the nations divided in the earth after the flood." Here is a roster of the human race so complete and so reliable that Augustine was ready to scoff at the possibility of inhabitants on the further side of the world, since no account was given of such in the table of Moses. The three sons of Noah had repeopled the earth. There were no antipodes, for all the peoples whose ancestors had landed from the original Mayflower, the Ark, were within hailing distance. This was the scheme and it was eminently satisfactory, and it may be said startlingly correct—within certain limits.

The tenth chapter of Genesis does not comprehend the entire human family. Lenormant contends for the unity of the race, but at the same time he says, "The descendants of the sons of Noah, so admirably catalogued by Moses, include one only of the races of humanity—the white race. The other races, the yellow, the red, the black, have no place in the Bible list of the nations sprung from Noah." And so associated with the theory that the flood was not universal is the hypothesis that other peoples besides the race of Adam existed at the time of this great convulsion. The marriage of Cain has been the *quodlibet* of theology, the stage property of the cheap critic, and the *bête noire* of the Bible class teacher ever since the poor fellow made that famous *mésalliance*. It is rarely introduced to the public except as a sort of *opéra bouffe,* where there is a desire to play to the galleries or to draw the crowd. Yet it may afford a glimmer of light in the gloom of the early dawn. It suggests that the Bible does not tell all it knows. The little stream of Scripture narrative trickles down some royal gorge or grand canyon of the dim and uncharted past, cabined, cribbed, confined, with only an occasional outward glimpse, and the world beyond, contemporaneous but unknown, may be desert or it may be the garden of the Lord.

The literary world allowed Milton to interpret the theogony of Genesis for many generations. It has allowed Byron to construe a perplexing verse of the same book.

In Gen. 6. 2 we read, "The sons of God saw the daughters of men that they were fair; and they took them wives of all which they chose." The poet has settled the meaning of these words, and the church has said neither yea nor nay. In Heaven and Earth Noah is made to say in the presence of Samiasa and Azaziel—angels, let us understand—

"These are they, then,
Who leave the throne of God to take of them wives
From out the race of Cain; the sons of heaven
Who seek earth's daughters for their beauty."

This has been the popular interpretation of the strange verse. And yet the usages of the language permit us to understand that the sons or servants of the gods, that is, the idolaters, intermarried with the daughters of the Adamite, that is, the race of Adam.

The author of the tenth chapter of Genesis is not to blame if he does not include in his classification the cave men of Europe, the Aztecs of Mexico, the fish-eaters of Australia. Perhaps he did not know of their existence actual or prospective. Perhaps it was not his purpose to mention them even if he did know. The written history of the world has been a history of the family of

UNITY OF THE RACE 61

Noah. The hoary old kingdom of China looks over her shoulder upon an unbroken stretch of centuries, but her influence has been slight upon general history. There is no Chinese blood in the veins of the dominant races. The same may be said of other peoples. They have contributed but little to the general fund. Their records are but partially read, their habitat has been circumscribed, they have not been related to the vigor and verve of the world. Here, then, in this luminous chapter we have an index of the world life. By a stroke of genius or by the light of inspiration the writer catalogues and classifies the makers of history. The heroes whose deeds have thrilled through a hundred generations; the poets and philosophers and philanthropists, the lawmakers and swordbearers, whose names have been inscribed upon stone and whose memory has been embalmed in song, and whose will has mapped out kingdoms—these are all here in embryo. But it is the prospectus of one great clan only.

Evidently we must look elsewhere than in the Bible for our ethnology, even as we look elsewhere for our geology and our physics. And so we have a linguistic ethnology, which talks sagely of the Aryan, the Semitic, and the

Turanian races. The Anglo-Saxon under the dome of Saint Paul's or amid the prairies of the middle West speaks of *seven* days in the week. The Russian moujik, drinking his vodka and growling at the starosta in his winter-bound village amid the Urals, calls it *sem*. The Persian, lounging under the palm groves of Ispahan, says *sab*. The Greek, as he climbed the marble steps of the Acropolis, said *hepta*. The Hindu, poring over his Veda by the snow-fed Indus, found the word written *saptan*. Here was one family, the Aryan or Indo-Germanic.

Between this and the Semitic stock there is the most extraordinary difference. At the same time the Semitic tongue is coherent and classifiable. It is the Turanian that has proved itself a maverick. It will not submit to branding. It is a linguistic salmagundi, a philological *omnium gatherum,* and its capricious irregularities have compelled anthropologists to abandon this method of classification. Moreover, it was found that there is no necessary connection between the race and the language. A people may change their language as easily as they revise their customs. The Normans dropped the Teutonic and adopted the French, carrying the latter

Unity of the Race 63

language into England and making linguistic confusion. There are conquering languages as there are conquering races.

Another attempt to classify the race is by a tabulation based upon the color of the skin. Three races are thus put in evidence: the ruddy, the brown, and the black. And the startling thing about this scheme is that all the sons of Noah are reckoned in the first class. And another startling thing is that Adam is held to belong to this class; and that if we are looking for race unity we must look further back than Adam. This is in perfect harmony with the hypotheses noted above in reference to the tenth chapter of Genesis. Moreover, we are told that this need not disconcert our mind nor bewilder our orthodoxy; since Adam or the first man of the ruddy race was the flowering or the climax of the prehistoric brown race; that ages before this the primitive black race had culminated in the progenitor of the brown people.

It is thus that the latest science talks of a common origin of the human race. Whether we go back by routes orthodox or liberal, scriptural or scientific, we reach one Rome to which all ancestral roads seem to lead. The last proclamation of the most fearless science is in harmony with the Old Testament Christ whose mission was to a world. The prophet looking beyond the limitations of his own people and the prejudices of his cradle faith says: "I saw in the night visions, and, behold, there came with the clouds of heaven one like unto a son of man, and he came even unto the ancient of days and they brought him near before him. And there was given him dominion, and glory, and a kingdom, that all the peoples, nations, and languages should serve him." And twentieth-century science, overturning the chauvinism of the ancient creeds and courageously questioning traditional orthodoxy, brings its latest findings and lays them at the feet of the Universal King; for all are of one stock, and the Son of man is the rightful sovereign since he is born of the blood.

It will be seen that those who contend for a succession of beginnings do not thereby exclude the earlier races from the plan of salvation in Jesus Christ. If the atonement possessed retroactive elements and reached back to Adam, why might it not go still further until it reaches the fountain head of universal humanity. If it has broken down the middle wall of partition between the Jew and the

Gentile may it not break down other barriers and overleap other bounds

> "Till earth's remotest nation
> Has learned Messiah's name."

Larger conceptions than this have been held. Sir David Brewster speaking of the redemptive scheme says, "Emanating from the middle planet of the system, why may it not have extended to them all—to the planetary races in the past when 'the day of their redemption had drawn nigh,' and to the planetary races of the future when 'their fullness of time shall come'?" Bishop Marvin writes, "We should expect to find it [the atonement] a central fact reaching in its effect the utmost limit of being in space and duration." These quotations are given to show that those who may claim a multiplicity of races are not necessarily committed to a limited redemption, since it has been seriously and calmly suggested that extramundane salvation may be wrought by the present scheme.

The universal phenomenon of a moral nature has been accepted as demonstrating race unity. Tribes have been found without temples or cities or schools, but they have not been found without the sense of ought. Some things are

right and some are wrong in the palace or in the
jungle. Laws are written on stone or papyrus or
paper or hearts, but they are written. We shall not
stop to inquire as to the origin of this sense
of duty. Whether it be grounded in expectation of reward, as Paley and Warburton would
imply, in the fear of punishment, according
to Professor Bain, or in a recognition of law,
according to Kant, it is here and it is to be
reckoned with. Jean Valjean, ex-convict,
mayor, and benefactor of the town in which
he lives, learns of a trial in which he is profoundly interested. An old man is about to
be sent to the galleys as Jean Valjean. A
storm rages in his soul. Shall he remain quiet
and allow matters to take their course? For
page after page we read the burning lines as
Victor Hugo leads us through the tragedy.
Questions of expediency, questions of casuistry, questions of honor, sweep through the
brain of the tortured man. Waking he destroys all proofs of his identity. Sleeping he
enters in a dream the village of Romainville,
where lilacs grow in April. But the sky is
gray, the houses are empty, and the city is still.
Jean Valjean is struggling with the sense of
ought.

A native servant in Australia loses his

wife. He asks of his master the privilege to go to a distant tribe, and there, according to custom, kill a woman in compensation for the life of his wife. The request is denied and he is threatened with punishment if he attempt to carry out his purpose. For months he pines and grows thin. He too is struggling with the sense of ought. He is seeking to compromise with his conscience. He is fighting the battle in the dark so vividly described by Victor Hugo's pen of fire. One day he disappears. He is gone for more than a year. He comes back cheerful and happy. No evidence can be secured except certain hints dropped by his second wife, but it is regarded as morally certain that he has put his plan into execution. He has obeyed the inner voice. He belongs to the same family with Jean Valjean. The Indian Thug who was filled with remorse when dying that he had not robbed and strangled as many strangers as his father had; the Italian coachman who murdered a lady whom he was taking to a country picnic, devoured the contents of her lunch basket, and then confessed to the priest that he had committed a sin by eating meat on Friday—these moral monstrosities reveal kinship with Cranmer, who held his hand in the flames until it fell from the blackened wrist because it had signed the recantation; and with Dr. Johnson, who stood all day long in the market place at Litchfield because years before he had refused to keep his father's bookstall.

"Yet still there whispers the small voice within,
Heard through gain's silence and o'er glory's din.
Whatever creed be taught or land be trod,
Man's conscience is the oracle of God."

But there is more in human nature than a sense of obligation. There is more or less defined a realization of responsibility to an unseen Power; and it is this which lies at the base of the sense of ought. This is the substratum of religion. Froude defines religion as a sense of responsibility to the Power that made us. Kant declares that "Religion consists in recognizing all our duties as divine commands." Here is the blossoming out of the sense of ought. When vague and indirect it constitutes the moral sense, when directed toward some Power as the object of responsibility it becomes religion. As thus conceived religion is not an invention of demagogues, a device of cunning priests wherewith to awe and control the masses. Certain accessories of religious worship or ecclesiastical observance may have thus their origin. They are mere party whips. Religion did not originate in tradition, since the tradition itself must originate. The first morning must have a dawn. It did not spring from ancestor worship, however beautiful may be that theory. Heathen nations usually end by worshiping gods in human form; the beginnings of their theology are more abstract and more elevated. Egyptian, Indian, Scandinavian mythologies are cleaner the farther back you go. Mediæval Mariolatry came after primitive Christianity. Religion is not the result of curiosity; it is not an inference of the intellect. Man learns to pray before he learns to reason. He looks for the footsteps of God among the stars and hears his trailing garments in the winds that whisper through the pines before he forms the first notion of cause and effect, or entertains the crudest ideas of design in creation. Religion is the attitude of the soul toward the God who reveals himself in the soul. It belongs to the soul. It belongs to every soul. It is the heritage of the race. It makes the race one.

These revelations of God may be more or less definite. They may be supplemented by verbal record, or by apprehension of natural phenomena. But the testimony of the Book or of nature is only supplementary and subsequent. It only indorses the inner voice, interprets its message, and enlarges its vocabulary. Men are worshiping animals even as they are thinking animals. Nobody asks the origin of hunger. It is an attribute of our physical being, a postulate of continued existence. Why, then, ask the origin of religion? God was not invented. Man is born religious as he is born hungry. His first impulse has been to get down on his knees and his next has been to lift his eyes toward the skies, and the question of the eyes and of the heart has been, "Who art Thou whose whispering I hear in my secret soul? Reveal thyself, that I may know thee. Uncover thy face, that I may see thee. Tell me thy name, that I may worship thee." No nation has been found in which there is no recognition of a Power that makes for right or wrong; and the rustle of the forest leaves, the moan of the uneasy sea, the blast of the storm trumpet, have been as the beckoning and signaling in the dark of an unspeakable Personality who seemed most likely to be able to satisfy the hunger of the soul.

Moreover, man is not only a moral being;

not only is he naturally religious, but he is universally susceptible to the appeals of the gospel. He is universally salvable by the atonement in Christ. Jesus has proved himself to be the desire of all nations. The heathen have been given to him as an inheritance and the uttermost parts of the earth as a possession. "Behold, these have come from far: and, lo, these from the north and from the west; and these from the land of Sinim." There is something about the Christ of the present-day thinking that meets the wants of the race, and that something is foreshadowed in the oldest faiths on record. The unity of the race was not emphasized by the writers of the Old Testament, but the Redeemer of the race was promised, and a redemption outlined that is possible to all. And so in these latter days the practice of the gospel keeps pace with the preaching of science. Ethnology outlines its theorem, while Christianity furnishes the demonstration. The race is one according to the analysis of the schools, the race is one in the programme of the church.

A representative of Christianity went to Sierra Leone in 1816. The remnants of thirty African tribes had been stranded there; the refuse of slave ships, the battered debris of a degraded humanity, besotted by drink, polluted by lust, maddened by violence. In eighteen months from the landing of the missionary a genuine Pentecost came with its religious fervor and heavenly uplift, and in seven years the community had become a model state. Jerome saw the Scots devouring human flesh. "Though there were plenty of cattle and sheep at their disposal, yet they preferred a ham of the herdsman or a slice of the female breast as a luxury." By means of the gospel of Christ these cannibals have blossomed into a Robert Burns or a Christopher North or a Dr. Chalmers or a John Hall. Charles Darwin visited the lower coast of South America, and wrote: "The Fuegians are in a more miserable state of barbarism than I had expected ever to have seen a human being. In this inclement country they are absolutely naked. As they threw their arms wildly around their heads, their long hair streaming, they seemed more like troubled spirits of another world." This was in 1833. Allan Gardiner went to these people with the gospel, and in a few years they had organized a society among themselves to rescue shipwrecked sailors.

In 1870 Darwin wrote Sir James Sullivan that the success of the mission among these

UNITY OF THE RACE 73

savages was "most wonderful, and shames me, as I always prophesied utter failure. I shall feel proud if your committee think fit to elect me an honorary member of your society." As a testimonial to his confidence in the work of the missionaries he inclosed a check for twenty-five dollars to the fund. The lowest race on earth had been discovered to be human by the Ithuriel spear of the Christ message. Even they could understand. The Archbishop of Canterbury, speaking at the annual meeting of the South American Missionary Society in 1885, said that the society "drew the attention of Charles Darwin and made him in his pursuit of the wonders of the kingdom of nature realize that there was another kingdom just as wonderful and more lasting."

This capacity to receive and to appropriate the gospel is the nexus that binds the race as a whole; that proves humanity to be a unit. Pliny set out to classify the animal creation, and he divided it into sea beasts, and earth beasts, and air beasts. Aristotle was more acute when he said there were but two kinds of animals, the blood-holding and the bloodless, or the *Enæma* and the *Anæma*. Two thousand years later Linnæus divided them into "beasts, birds, amphibians, fish, insects, and worms." Even Linnæus did not look below the surface. He judged by external form. He was deceived by appearances. To-day classification is based not upon shape or color or habitat, but upon structure. And so we hear of the great order of Vertebrata, the backbone family, and everything with a backbone belongs to that family. What if it be a fish and dwell in the caverns of the sea; what if it be a reptile and glide through the ooze of the swamp; what if it be a bat and whirl through the gloom of the night; what if it be an ape and mow on its perch in the park; what if it be an emperor whose word is the law of millions? Science, the social democrat, has said to all, "Ye are kindred." The spinal column is there. This articulated elastic chain of bones binds together the high and the low, the clean and the unclean, the upright and the prone, into one great family. Every other classification is false. So is any classification of the human race based upon color or speech or culture. It may serve as a convenient gauge for practical use, but it is not the last analysis. Not the skin, not the brain, but the heart marks man as man. And wherever there is a heart that responds to the love of Christ there is a member of the great family for

UNITY OF THE RACE

whose material good the world was made, and for whose spiritual rescue the Creator died.

And so, whatever may be the findings of a radical and revolutionary science, however much our cradle faiths may be jarred and our family circle broken by the restless intruder Evolution, the truth still abides that we are brothers. This is not the result of civilization but the basis of civilization. Men do not learn this as they grow enlightened, but there can never be the highest enlightenment until men start with this as a premise. The lesson is a large one. We have been taught by our theological masters that God had but one Son; that men unsaved are merely animals and when saved merely adopted children. That there is no spiritual blood relationship with those beyond the territory of regeneration. We do not believe all this now. We have learned to call Jesus the great Elder Brother; not mine but ours, not sectional but ethnic. Men of every race, of every moral grade, of every theological creed, are the sons of a King —prodigal sons, let us say, but sons; and regeneration is the stripping of the rags, the purging from the swine pens, the reseating at the table. Change of heart? Yes. Change of nature? Yes. But not change of blood nor change of lineage. "For Thou art our Father, though Abraham knoweth us not, and Israel doth not acknowledge us: thou, O Lord, art our father; our redeemer from everlasting is thy name."

With this message we go to the world. It is God's world filled with God's men and women. They, not God, need to be reconciled. They, not God, need to remember their relationship. And it is this great truth which appears here and there in the old dispensation that is coming more and more to the front as we get back to Bethlehem and the Christ.

IV

THE DEVELOPMENT OF THE RACE

IV

The Development of the Race

A RECENT writer has said that church history moves not in straight lines, but in cycles not always symmetrical, but more or less definite, and each cycle consisting of four segments. These segments he calls the mystical, the doctrinal, the scholastic, and the critical. In the mystical period "the truth is held in solution." In the doctrinal it is "precipitated and takes visible form." In the scholastic the molten doctrine has been "run into molds and has settled into cast-iron shape." And then comes the time when men, growing weary of forms, "go back to elementary facts" and reëxamine foundations; this is the critical period. The first is the age of Saint John; the second is the age of Chrysostom; the third is the age of Thomas Aquinas; the last is the age of Erasmus. Then begins another cycle. The mystical period is represented by Jacob Boehme in Germany and by Madame Guyon in France. The doctrinal era finds worthy exponents in the Puritans and Scotch Covenanters. Then came Leibnitz and Spinoza and Lessing, who may fairly be said to represent the scholastic stage; and then the critical era—introduced by the textual criticism of the Bible by Kennicott, Griesbach, and others, and supplemented by what Eichhorn was pleased to call "higher criticism," to distinguish it from the linguistic and philological study of the book.

For a generation past we have been living in the critical segment of the cycle. It is the climacteric period, the aphelion point of the orbit where the flying body gathers itself for the return toward the center, the ebb of the night when animate and inanimate nature with a weird thrill of expectancy turns its face toward the east. There is reason to believe that another cycle is about to begin, that we are on the threshold of another mystical era. German rationalism is less positive in its findings. A radical American has already asked in some perturbation if Professor Harnack has not gone to Canossa. Professor Armstrong, of Wesleyan, writes of the return to faith, and says that the "era of doubt is drawing toward its close." The watchword of the day is, "Back to Christ," and a glance at the newest book suggests that the trend toward a moderate pietism is a sign of the times; a marked evangelism indeed seems imminent.

These periods are not so much cycles, after all, as spirals of progress—a sort of evolutionary switchback railroad on which the train apparently returns again and again to the same point but each time higher up the slope, a change of altitude rather than a change of latitude. It is the struggle of Christianity with the inertia of the race; it is the natural ferment of the truth, and is inevitable when we consider the problem of race evolution to be solved and the character of the great faith by which the work is to be done. Moreover, its consideration throws some light on the theological unrest which is so marked in the best thinking of the day.

Christianity is essentially constructive. It creates. Whatever it touches it improves. It destroys only to reproduce in better form. It permits the seed to die as the condition and the prophecy of harvest. John the Baptist came—rugged, fierce, declamatory—and said, "Now also the ax is laid unto the root of the trees;" and the world waited and watched for the divine Woodman. But the mission of Jesus was not "to destroy, but to fulfill." There was much that was wrong, many radical changes to be made; but it was correction and not destruction, fruition and not annihilation, that was needed. Thus the Master said, "Among them that are born of women there hath not risen a greater than John the Baptist: notwithstanding he that is least in the kingdom of heaven is greater than he." John was a destroyer. He declared war upon existing religious conditions. He thundered against the hypocrisy of the day; and, clothed in camel's hair and disdaining all luxuries, he dwelt a hermit in the desert. There was only one way to cure the evils of the time, and that was by unquenchable fire. This was his theory of reformation, and his idea of the imminent reformer. So, when the Messiah had come and the world moved on undisturbed and political conditions remained unchanged, a great doubt oppressed the Baptist, and out from his prison came the momentous inquiry, "Art thou he that should come, or do we look for another?" John was in theory a destroyer, but Christianity is not a system of destruction. The least of those who have caught its constructive spirit, who are filled with the instinct of growth, whose ambition is to lift, to enlarge, to exalt, is in so far greater than the great forerunner who plowed deep the furrow but had not the seed ready with which to fecundate the waiting soil.

No scheme can flourish on a "Thou shalt not." No system of destructive criticism can ever be incorporated and abide. The world wants more than negation. Agnosticism, which, according to Frederick Harrison, is "the belief that there is a sort of something about which we can know nothing," can never be the conquering creed. Alaric and Genghis Khan and Tamerlane are not of the world's heroes. The world prefers a Robinson Crusoe, building his hut in the thicket and making the wilderness fruitful, or a Robert Clive, who gave India to Great Britain and daybreak to India.

In the constructive process Christianity has sought everywhere for material and for plans. It lays the world of thought and of motive under contribution. The Bible contains the word of God, but it does not contain all of that word. It does not claim to possess it all. On the contrary, it constantly refers us to other sources of knowledge and of truth. The heavens declare the glory of God, as well as the book. Paul testifies that God has not "left himself without witness," even where there is no Bible, "in that he did good, and gave us rain from heaven, and fruitful seasons." Coleridge is not a heretic when he says:

> "Believe that every bird that sings,
>   And every flower that stars the elastic sod,
> And every breath the radiant summer brings,
>   To the pure spirit is a word of God."

Jesus calls the lilies and the sparrows to give testimony, and God is ready to refer his controversy with Job to the war horse, the leviathan, or to the swing of Orion and Arcturus. These things were before there were any Scriptures. There is the truth of God and there is the purpose of God revealed constantly in history. The daily papers contain his marching orders. The nations of the world are our schoolmasters to lead us unto Christ. Every fragment of figured clay from the mounds of Chaldea, every page of lettered papyrus, every hieroglyph of hoary Egypt is a fresh installment of the message of God to man.

Christianity has drawn from all these sources. It stands ready to correlate all these truths. It is not ashamed to pick up a gem from the mire. It is not afraid to appropriate a great truth, even though it be born and bred in the haunts of great errors. It has heeded the counsel of Lowell written in a copy of Omar Khayyam:

> "Where Doubt's eddies toss and whee!
> Faith's slender shallop till her footing reel,
> Plunge! If you find not peace beneath the whirl,
> Groping you may like Omar grasp a pearl."

Philo, the Alexandrian philosopher, sought to harmonize the Mosaic and the Platonic philosophies, and adopted the word "Logos." This word is intended to mean the embodiment of the divine powers. It is impersonal; it is unintelligible; it is misleading. Out of it came the formidable gnostic heresy. It was a dangerous word to handle, as it was full of unexplored possibilities. Yet Christianity caught it, domesticated it, and it became the shibboleth of the fourth gospel, the sign manual of John the Beloved. As a religious symbol the cross is prehistoric. There was a cross on the great glass image of Serapis brought from the Black Sea three centuries before Christ, and the priests of Egypt begged that it might be spared as it was the emblem of their god and of the life to come. The Spanish missionaries found the natives of America worshiping the cross. It is engraved upon the oldest temples in Mexico and Central

America—buildings of unknown antiquity. It was called the "key of the Nile" by which Osiris opened the fountains of the south and poured the life-giving river over the land. "Thor's Hammer," as it is called, found on ancient stones in the far north, is but a rude figure of the cross. The old Viking made a sign of the hammer over the meat offered at sacrifice; it was the sign of the cross in crude and initial form. Egypt, Assyria, China, Scandinavia have thus antedated Christianity in the use of its most sacred symbol, and Christianity has not disdained to accept that which comes fragrant with the mystery of a world-wide reverence and hallowed with the associations of countless centuries.

The pagan father in Norway received the infant, and, if he decided to preserve it, poured water over it and gave it a name. To destroy its life after that was murder. The child had been initiated into civil life—it had been baptized. And this, centuries before the first infant received its Christian name on the application of water and was thus initiated into the church. Was there an exalted precept of Greek philosophy or a pregnant line of Greek poetry, it became a part of the message of this new religion to the world. Was there a suggestive Roman custom or a worthy Roman law, it has come down to us wearing the livery of the Christian faith.

Thus is prepared a system thoroughly equipped to become the efficient cause of race evolution. It is a specific compounded of the best ingredients. It is a piece of machinery in which are combined all the latest improvements. Its appeal is found to be ever fresh and new, and its tendency is always to construct and to dignify. For instance, it reveals God—a God large enough for the growing wants of the race, a God who by his essential nature helps the race to grow and gives it room in which to grow. In him we are led out into a large place. He is uncreated. He is infinite. He is the author of the past and the arbiter of the future. He is himself a builder, and whatever goes forth from his hand carries in it the impulse and spirit of development. This religious scheme reveals life—not merely the play of emotions, the enterprise of trade, the interchange of greetings which make our diary record, but the larger life as it stands related to the universe; the end of the path which has been left out of sight behind, and the end which is not yet on the horizon ahead. We are not strangers to ourselves, when we have listened to the teachings of Christianity; we are not strangers and pilgrims on the earth, as were the old patriarchs. It is Immanuel's land, and it belongs to us none the less because we go hence, by and by. We have learned why we are here, and the path that leads hence when the school is over.

There are religions and religions. Some keep men as they are. There is no stir, no progress. The dead hand is on the brakes. The will of the fathers is the way of the children, and life stagnates. Other religions are distinctly evil. They encourage vice. They pander to the lowest instincts; indeed, they make the perversion of these instincts a religious service, and bring man in his devotions —in fact, by his devotions—to lower levels. Idolatry manufactures its gods, and gives them "few of the attributes of heaven and all of the attributes of earth." They are usually inhuman, rather than superhuman. "Think of Buddha and you become Buddha" is Chinese, and it is also psychology. If the life is to be exalted the object worshiped must be superior to the worshiper. Hinduism and Buddhism offer no help in this world, and Confucianism offers none in the world to come. Mohammedanism knows nothing better than the sword as an evangelizing agency, and nothing higher than sense as the motive or reward of service. But Christianity puts man on the upward path, shows him the sun blaze on the summit, fills his soul with longing, and wings his feet with hope; then it keeps step with him upward into the light. In the struggle for supremacy between flesh and spirit Christ's Christianity is never on the earth side. It does not degrade the body; it glorifies it by making it subordinate. It does not destroy sense, it directs it.

The effect of this is to magnify the individual. The value of human life is a modern discovery. It was the cheapest commodity in the market until quite recently. And that not only in pagan lands—in Rome, where the flesh of slaves was used to fatten the fish for the patrician table; in the Fiji Islands, where a life was sacrificed whenever a canoe was launched; in Dahomey, where the living wives were buried with broken legs in the pit with their dead husband—but in England, and even in America. England executed three hundred beggars in one year for asking alms. To shoot a rabbit in the New Forest of William I was to be hanged or boiled alive. To cut down a tree in an orchard, to steal property to the value of five shillings from a shop or forty shillings from a dwelling house, to break through a window and take goods at five o'clock in the afternoon, to counterfeit the stamp used as a tax on hair powder—this meant death. To stay away thrice from church was a capital offense in old Virginia.

It is the modern Christ who emphasizes the greater value of a man than a sheep. In the days of his incarnation Jesus tried to teach that the hairs of the head are numbered, that all heaven sympathized with the return of a single sinner, that one sheep on the mountains at nightfall meant distress and confusion through all the household and a night of unrest and wandering on the part of the shepherd. But the world forgot all this, and is only recently bringing it to mind. During the late war with Spain a crowd stood in front of one of the great metropolitan newspaper offices reading the changing bulletins. A little fellow had been dressed as an American sailor and placed upon the scaffold where he could walk back and forth in full sight. Suddenly he stumbled and fell. A cry of dismay went up from the crowd, and one man, rough-handed, brown-faced, rude-mannered, cried out, with more or less of unreportable expletives, "Catch him quick, he's worth more than the whole newspaper!" The ancestors of that man would have left the boy out in the forest to die, if it had not suited their fancy to maintain him. The famous line, "I am a man, and whatsoever concerns humanity concerns me," when first uttered on a Roman stage brought the whole audience to their feet with shouts of applause. Yet the man in the play who gives expression to such a noble sentiment is the father who a little earlier had complained because his wife exposed one of their children, instead of killing it as he had commanded.

Abraham prepared to put Isaac to death without any scruples of conscience. His father-heart was broken, his faith in God's promise that in Isaac the earth should be blessed was shaken, but there is no reason to believe that there was any question in his mind from the ethical standpoint. To-day the moral complexion of such a sacrifice would be argued as proof that the command did not come from God. Abraham had no such problem to solve, as his valuation of human life was vastly different from that which now obtains.

Wherever Christianity has been permitted to proclaim its whole message it has taught that life is sacred. The Spanish Inquisition, the horrors perpetrated in the Netherlands, the atrocities of Cortes and Pizarro were made possible by first crippling the true faith. One of the surgeons of the Charity Hospital, Stockholm, experimented at first upon calves with the virus of smallpox. But this was expensive, and, according to his own declaration, he eventually used children as subjects, since children were cheaper than calves. In the Vienna hospital experiments were made upon the hapless patients with hyoscyamine sulphate, while the tortured victims would again and again beg on bended knees for death as a relief from their suffering. Here, Christianity was virtually discarded, and a dead materialism took its place. Men and women are only animals. And this is science, whose "sweet reasonableness" is so often pledged to check the despotism of the church, unlock the fetters of tradition, and preach the brotherhood of man. All these atrocities are perpetrated in this sacred name. Not a perversion of science, but a science without religion—a cold, planning brain, an unsanctified intellect, a lawless corsair steel-prowed and armor-clad that ranges the seas, obedient to no orders, owing no allegiance, carrying no flag, ready to ride down anything that crosses its path of discovery or conquest. Christianity founded these hospitals and now pleads to control them, and, when it does, experiments with living human flesh to gratify curiosity or to establish some personal dictum will cease, for the body is the temple of the Holy Ghost.

A religious scheme that develops the individual gives the race better leaders, and the race has come into its kingdom largely through leadership. Men of power are more than a product of their times, they are the producers as well. They represent in the beginning the best possible raw material, before it has been wrought upon by the machinery; in the end they improve the machinery. The times help to develop them, and they enrich the times so that the next evolution is yet larger and better. The history of the race cannot be written if we leave biography out. It will be full of impassable gaps. Greek philosophy is terra incognita without Socrates and Aristotle. Charlemagne is another name for mediæval Europe. It has been said that "time was the parent and silence was the nurse of the British Constitution"; yet the growth of that majestic unwritten instrument cannot be noted without a study of the lives of Sir Matthew Hale, Lord Somers, and others. Christianity trains leaders. It brings out the best in the individual. It shows him, indeed, that there is a best in him. It plants the first seed of self-respect in the heart, and stands guard over the field as the harvest matures. It makes the man who makes other men. It stimulates to the best endeavor those who become a stimulus to others. It is the normal class where the teachers of the world are in training.

But it deals also with the rank and file. Its mission is not only to the man on the bridge, but also to the man behind the gun. In its leavening of the individual Christianity leavens the whole lump. The crowd is only an aggregation of individuals, the race is only a confederation of units. If each man is of the blood royal it is a race of kings. The religion of Osiris built obelisks written all over with silly compliments to the reigning Pharaoh, and pyramids in which one man was buried and in the construction of which thousands of other men died under the lash. The religion of Jesus Christ builds in that same land a giant dam across the Nile, by which thousands of acres are to be irrigated and hundreds of thousands are to be fed. Rome called its inns *hospitalia,* and lodged there the favored guest; Christianity calls them "hospitals," and means either a place for medical treatment or an asylum for the poor. Christianity denies the theory of Epicurus and Lucretius, that the gods never interfere with life on this earth, that the concerns of the world do not affect them, that they dwell within

> "The lucid interspace of world and world,
> Where never creeps a cloud nor moves a wind,
> Nor sound of human sorrow mounts to mar
> Their sacred everlasting calm."

Its pleasure is to reveal to us a God who looks after the grass of the field, and provides for the ravens that venture upon the shelterless winter without storehouse or barn. When the barbarians came down upon Italy and the race seemed to be swept from its moorings Christianity put herself at the head of these savage world-breakers, taught them how to form stable governments, and led them into the path of progress. When the dark ages followed, as a result of this overthrow of order, and learning was about to be buried in the ruins of the cities and kingdoms that went down in the track of Genseric and Attila, Christianity opened her cathedral schools and trained her priests and monks to keep the "fires of literature burning by the side of the fires of the altar." When that learning seemed destined to become the heritage of the rich and leisured classes only, Christianity taught Gutenberg how to carve his movable types, and prompted Luther to break the dead hand of the obsolete languages and turn the Bible loose in the mother tongue.

The result of all this may now be clearly seen. The development of the individual means the overthrow of feudalism, civil or ecclesiastical. There are still traces of mediævalism in theological opinion and relics of feudalism in ecclesiastical polity, but they are doomed by the law of the survival of the fittest. This, of course, implies revolution, as well as evolution, and revolutions destroy many an ancient landmark and disturb many a night's slumber. It means the birth of modern criticism, but since Christianity is the foster mother of criticism we need not fear that the latter will ever become a matricide. Out of this uplift have come Columbus and Magellan and Da Gama in discovery; Bacon and Descartes and Darwin in science; Luther and Savonarola and Wesley in religion; Delitzsch and De Wette and Driver in exegesis. Out of it has come modern history, where every man has a right to look for the truth. And the honest quest of truth and its fearless announcement when discovered are the surest safeguards against the reactionary forces, ever in evidence, that would block the wheels of progress, stagnate the currents of evolution, and stay the sunrise that is breaking over the world.

V

ARRESTED DEVELOPMENT—
MILITARISM

V

Arrested Development—Militarism

THE world is waiting for the peacemaker. The millenniums of militarism have wearied the race of strife. The fight has gone on since the dawning of organic life. Indeed, before there was life the action and interaction of cosmic forces were a fitting prelude to the struggle that was inaugurated when the first cell quivered with the vital germ. The ocean bed is strewn with battered fragments of the solid land, and the mountain peak will show you shells and sea fossils, the trophies won from the deep. The rivers came down from the hills, cutting deep channels as they came, and now spend their strength in chafing against their self-made barriers and trying to get out of bounds. All over our Northern states are scattered bowlders, "lost rocks," that have been dragged away from their home in the stress of world growth, and will never get back again. The Churchill Rock in New Hampshire weighs six thousand tons and came from the Hudson Bay. The porphyry bowlder of

Saint Ignace, Michigan, has no kindred south of far Canada. In the grapple of giants these fugitives were torn from their family groups. The march of the glacier brought them south and left them lonely and forgotten.

Life came to share with matter the heritage of conflict; to measure swords with matter for standing room and forage; to wage ceaseless internecine war for the perpetuation of species. In this succession came man. "To your tents, O Israel," has been his rallying cry from the beginning. He must prove his right to exist and prove it against all comers. The elements were in the list. The cold, the heat, the storm, the drought sent in their cartel. He must run the shifting gauntlet of the turncoat year. He fought for food, for the fishing streams and hunting grounds. He fought for his wife, his children, his clan. He is fighting still, and there are those who teach that he must go on fighting to the end. To them there is no lesson in evolution, no ultimate good to the race. What has been will be, and will be because it has been.

It is said that war kindles patriotism; that a man never realizes his love for the flag until it is afield; that the rattle of the drum in the street awakens all his latent loyalty; that in

ARRESTED DEVELOPMENT 103

the grave of dead heroes a nation buries its sectionalism and partisanship. There is a sense in which this is true. The war with France made a united Germany and crowned the king of Prussia German emperor. The recent war with Spain rubbed out the Mason and Dixon's line, sent cowboy and banker to sleep under the same tent, and made "The Star-Spangled Banner" a national song. Yet the truest patriotism is opposed to war. Dr. Johnson called patriotism "the refuge of the scoundrel." He had in mind a certain not unusual brand of the article in question, and he knew what he was saying. The demagogism that shouts for war expecting it to become the arena for personal glory; the Ishmaelitism whose hand is against every man's hand; the jingoism that always carries a chip on its shoulder; the chauvinism that cannot see across the national boundary—these are sometimes called patriotism and go into the lists with blare of trumpet and beat of drum. But genuine patriotism is not compounded of such stuff.

The intelligent patriot knows that the good of his country is involved in the general good of mankind; that the best interests of his own land lie not in slaughtering nations, but in selling to them. At New Haven in 1898, during the Spanish War, William H. Taft, later Secretary of War, said: "There are several kinds of patriotism. We heard in Alumni Hall this morning of that quiet, self-denying patriotism which is working for the good of all in securing better government, and which has not the plaudits of the crowd and the deep gratitude of the people before it as a reward for labor and self-sacrifice. In the long run this kind works more for the good of the country than any other. It needs not the spur of palpable danger or the excitement and fervor of war's alarms to arouse it. It is a constant force making for public righteousness."

Indeed, war tends sooner or later to the stifling of the truest patriotism. It paves the way for the despot. Against the background of powder clouds appears so often the dim figure of "the man on horseback." The man whose word is supreme in the camp may practice dictation in the market place. There can be no method in the march nor in battle without absolute authority, and the same authority may extend to civil life; will naturally affect civil life if the latter be saturated with militarism. Herbert Spencer cites the

ARRESTED DEVELOPMENT

case of ancient Peru under the control of the militant Incas. The nation was enslaved. The clothing worn by the different classes was prescribed, and the dining room door must be kept open so that the judges might enter at any moment. "To live in Germany at the present time is like returning to the nursery," says a recent writer. The civilian has no rights which the soldier is bound to respect. Any criticism of the Kaiser is lese-majesty and is treated as felony. The critic is not allowed bail and is brought to trial in prison dress—and all this since the Franco-Prussian War. War sooner or later stifles true patriotism by suggesting a false ideal to the patriot by cultivating national selfishness, by shutting his eyes to the excellencies found in other states, and by training him to a recognition of supreme authority that will paralyze his own individuality.

This leads to the consideration of another military sophism. M. Lavisse, in A General View of the Political History of Europe, says, "It is a question whether universal peace is a desirable object, whether it would not diminish the original energy of national genius." "The Private Soldier," writes Lord Wolseley, "must believe that his duties are the noblest that fall to man's lot. He must be taught to despise all those of civil life." Even Tennyson, the broad-spirited poet, lends his voice to the glorification of war, a war that reflected but little credit upon England:

"And the heart of the people beat with one desire,
For the peace, that I deemed no peace, is over and done,
And now by the side of the Black and the Baltic deep,
And deathful grinning mouths of the fortress, flames
The blood-red blossom of war with a heart of fire.
Let it flame or fade, and the war roll down the wind,
We have proved we have hearts in a cause, we are noble still,
And myself have awaked, as it seems, to a better mind;
It is better to fight for the good than to rail at the ill;
I embrace the purpose of God and the doom assigned."

So it is said again and again that war awakens energy and courage; that it develops the nobler qualities and gives inspiration to the race. Then why not have war for its own sake? If it be the only hero maker; if the national spirit would degenerate in its absence; if it be the only mainspring of racial evolution, why not organize a general congress whose jurisdiction shall cover all civilized people, and whose business it shall be to arrange for a war at stated intervals between selected nations, to continue during a prescribed number of months? This is good political economy. It would mean sorrow and woe to the few, but the welfare of the many would be enhanced. It would bring the greatest good to the greatest number. And when by judicious management and timely conflicts one people had grown too strong to find anywhere a foeman worthy of their steel, then plan for civil strife, foment internecine dissension, organize a revolution or two, split a nation into hostile camps, turn the sword of brother against brother, for this is the way to the heights.

This, however, is not the theory of European politics. The mighty armaments are not intended as agencies of evolution. War may be the school of the highest human qualities, the nurse of virtue, the gymnasium of racial energy, but it is not in the interest of evolution and social progress that the nations are armed to the teeth. It is a struggle for life, and instead of fostering the nobler qualities it really cripples the individual, makes him but part of a machine, posits him in the social organism, and limits his sphere of action as a unit. The plea of the peoples whose warships are afloat and whose soldiers are drilled is that all these things make for peace. Count Muravieff in behalf of the Russian Czar announces as the purpose of the Peace Congress, "to accept in principle the employment of the good offices of mediation and facultative arbitration in cases lending themselves thereto, with the object of preventing armed conflicts between nations." Why all this if war be necessary to cultivate the higher qualities of courage and self-reliance? The Czar said to the French President at a great military review in Saint Petersburg, "The Russian army and the French army constitute a real brotherhood of arms, which we can regard with all the greater satisfaction because these imposing forces are not destined to support one another aggressively, but, on the contrary, to strengthen the maintenance of general peace." But wherefore all this? If war be necessary to prevent reversion to type, why take away the occupation of the soldiers and thus interfere with racial development.

It is further claimed that war advances the national interests. There is indeed an almost universal sentiment entertained that we owe our national integrity and growth to the soldiers; that these ought to be the pride as they are the creators of the republic. This is the contention of a distinguished English general who said in public address, "The glorious possession which we inherit from our forefathers has been built up bit by bit by the glorious deeds, by the courage and valor, of her majesty's army and navy." It would be interesting to ask how much of the British empire has been built up by the army and navy. Certainly not England itself, with its factories, and fields, and mines, and shipyards. Certainly not the broad domain of Canada, nor the commonwealth of Australia, nor the islands of the sea. It is British thrift and not British gunpowder, British artisans and shopkeepers and explorers and missionaries and not British soldiers, that have followed the sun with the Union Jack, and girdled the globe with the English speech. It is only when the sword has been beaten into a plowshare that the desert is made to blossom as a rose. The soldiers have rather helped to disintegrate the work of the mechanics. The United States of America might to-day be a part of Great Britain if the soldiers could have been held off. India would break away in death and ruin if England had only soldiers to depend upon. The cartridges furnished by the military department for military purposes and greased with lard brought on the Sepoy rebellion that swept India with a tempest of blood. The military raid of Captain Jameson broke many a loving heart in England, and dug ten thousand graves along the bleak kopjes of South Africa. It meant the addition of a new province, but most likely this would have happened eventually without bloodshed.

So may it be said of the United States—not one inch of territory, not one advantage, gained by force of arms but might have been more cheaply and more honorably secured by other means. This is the testimony of U. S. Grant. He writes, "Though I have been trained as a soldier and have participated in many battles, there never was a time when, in my opinion, some way could not have been found to prevent the drawing of the sword"—one of the wisest leaders of modern times deprecating his own calling; one great general on record as saying, "War is hell;" another declaring, "War is a blunder." Our Revolutionary War was a glorious struggle—so say school histories and the July orators; but it was merely an outcome of the military idea dominant at the court of

George III. The war with Mexico was the attack of a brigand, who levies tribute because he is stronger. The civil war cost eight billions of dollars. The total wealth of the eleven seceding states was a little over five billions. The entire South could have been bought, plantations, cotton warehouses, negroes, and all, and three billions would have been saved—and no reckoning demanded for the slaughtered thousands, the broken homes, the paralyzed industries, the moral collapse, which make grewsome the history of that awful struggle.

When this war closed it left a number of delicate problems unsettled. One of these grew out of the equipment of Confederate cruisers in English ports. It was suggested that this matter be settled by arbitration. At once Lord Russell, the Foreign Secretary, refused. He maintained that the English people were the sole guardians of their own honor. It was a critical moment. The people of the United States, though wearied with the long strife, realized their strength as never before. A splendidly successful general was in the presidential chair. But a few months earlier fifty thousand men had been ready to start for the Mexican frontier to inquire as to the reason for the stay of a French army in the Mexican capital, and to suggest that its visit had been long enough. A war between England and America at this time would have been a struggle between giants, and if war is good it therefore would have been an inestimable benediction to the race. But the clear-sighted statesmanship of these two Christian nations did not indorse this fallacy. England indeed felt that fifteen million dollars levied by the Court of Arbitration was not an excessive price to pay for peace. The fact is that Europe pays four million dollars per day on her armaments in order to prevent war. Nothing conceivable would so advance the interests of Europe and of the world as the assurance that war had become an impossibility. It would bring the golden age. It would inaugurate an industrial millennium. It would quiet much of the feverish fluctuation of the market and make the poor man's savings safe.

A school of political economists has held that war is a prime factor in civilization; that universal peace would mean social and intellectual stagnation; that a peaceful nation is a hermit nation; isolation is fatal to progress; a people soon reaches the limit of native mental or industrial growth; variety of influence and environment alone can bring the largest results and assure the ripest maturity; it is not good for Moab to be at his ease from his youth and to settle on his lees—he needs to be emptied from vessel to vessel, and mayhap go into captivity. There is something in this. A casual reading of history would seem to establish this theory. War, God's enemy, has wrought God's work. "He maketh the wrath of man to praise him." This Saul with fingers of steel and eyes of flame is also among the prophets. More than once some Jeremiah has cried anew, "O thou sword of the Lord, how long will it be ere thou be quiet? put up thyself into thy scabbard; rest, and be still;" and the reply of a stern Providence has been, "How can it be quiet, seeing the Lord hath given it a charge?"

Men have fought against oppression and prejudice, against the thraldom of tradition and the tyranny of caste, and have come into the day. The history of liberty is a record of battles. Its first great Exponent came to bring a sword upon the earth, and its first great struggle was against the religious despotism of God's chosen people. John Stuart Mill was not ashamed to say, "A great crisis in the history of liberty seems to me to have come at the cross of Jesus of Nazareth." After years of struggle and of experimenting, Christian liberty—the other name for human liberty—adopted as its champion and *protégé* the wild, uncultured, but clean-blooded Saxon, the barbarian who held town meetings in the depths of the German forests and who ratified his laws by the shout of the people and the clash of shields.

Now let us read the history of England with this clue and what a luminous record it is! It is a log book of evolution. Fifty years ago historical records were but little more than court records. The rise and fall of dynasties, state ceremonies and military parades, the scheming of placemen, the intrigues of the back stairs, "the tedious pomp that waits on kings"—all this had been dignified with the name of history. Only in recent years has Green proposed A Short History of the English People, or Aubrey written The Rise and Growth of the English Nation. Walter Scott spent his splendid strength in Marmion, and The Lords of the Isles, and The Lady of the Lake, but Tennyson dares to glorify the Charge of the Light Brigade, and Kipling touches with wizard pencil the hanging of Danny Deever, and makes a place in the national heart and in the national Hall of Fame for Tommy Atkins, who is

> "Tommy this an' Tommy that an'
>   'Tommy, 'ow's your soul?'
> But it's 'thin red line of 'eroes' when
>   The drums begin to roll.
> For it's Tommy this an' Tommy that an'
>   'Chuck him out, the brute,'
> But it's 'saviour of 'is country' when
>   The guns begin to shoot."

Little by little the people have come to the front. They learned to fight, they learned to read, they learned to vote.

America has taken up the task. The War of the Revolution was a paradox and a revelation. It not only made the American people free, it made them want to be free. It resolved them to be free. Congress decided to raise an army to resist the encroachments of England. The same Congress also emphatically declared, "We do not mean to dissolve the union which has so long and so happily subsisted" between the English and the American peoples. The Declaration of Independence was the result, and not the cause, of the war. The war itself prepared the nation for the consequences of the war. The premature, explosive, declaration of the Scotch-Irish patriots of Mecklenburg County, North Carolina, investing the provincial Congress with "all legislative and executive power," came before any powder was burned. But this attracted local attention only. Not until the Hessian had been hired, and Boston had fallen into hostile hands, and a British fleet had pounded the palmetto logs of Fort Moultrie for ten long hours—only then was the old Statehouse bell struck, and a new creed sent forth as the rallying cry for the fighting millions of the race.

The war between the states was to defend the Constitution. It resulted in the emancipation of the negro. The Federal armies met with defeat until they got into the divine plan. God had no use for the armies of the North except as champions of the whole Declaration of Independence, and exponents of liberty. The end of 1862 was the dark period of the rebellion. But 1863 begun with a call for three times three hundred thousand men—and the Emancipation Proclamation. Both were held to be military necessities, but the latter was the moral condition which gave dignity and vigor to the former. This Proclamation lifted the conflict from the low ground of a struggle between factions, to a grapple of the forces that make for human good or ill. The Northern armies, without realizing it, were fighting for progress, for evolution, for to-morrow. The emancipation of the bondman was only an incident, only the local form in which the world-old struggle had materialized. It was the next step upward, and this step was taken over the bodies of the heroic Federal and Confederate dead.

Now, all this may be true. But times are changing. The old methods are crass and brutal. The king who orders a batch of prisoners beheaded to make divertisement for his tufthunters and court parasites belongs to the ape and elephant stage of evolution. The tribal clans that need to try conclusions on the battlefield in order to settle some question of polity or territory or international etiquette are only overgrown prizefighters. The nation that needs bloodshed as the condition of its best growth, that stagnates unless its flag is afield and its soldiers are killing, is out of step, and deserves to fall behind and be forgotten. Militarism is elemental. It is the Tartar hypostasis which may be discovered by scratching a Russian. Not more instinctively does the horse smell the battle afar off, and quiver at the thunder of the captains and the shouting, than does man glory in the military trappings and warlike parade that mean the destruction of his fellow men. King Henry at Harfleur was touching a popular chord when he said:

> "In peace there is nothing so becomes a man
> As modest stillness and humility.
> But when the blast of war blows in our ears,
> Then imitate the action of the tiger."

Here, then, is the secret of it all. It is a symptom of arrested development. The race is destined to outgrow this stage or this manifestation. It is on its way to a higher grade in the great evolution. Mr. Spencer defines an army as a mobilized community, and a community as an army at rest. The army stage of development precedes the community stage. First the hunter state, then the pastoral, then the agricultural—this is the scientific order, and only in the last is there permanency in values and integrity of institutions.

This transition is not to be made by any special form of government. Very early in the history of America it was claimed that the problem had been solved; that the genius of a republic is pacific, and the people would seek their best interests by avoiding war as self-destructive. Alexander Hamilton showed the fallacy of this claim. He pointed out that there had been almost as many popular as royal wars. Sparta, Athens, Rome, and Carthage were republics. Yet Sparta was but little better than a well regulated camp, and Carthage was the aggressor in the war that ended in her own destruction. Nor is the reform to be effected by the cultivation of commerce. Venice sent her trading ships into every sea, yet the war flag of this proud little island city was as well known as her merchant flag. No nation in Europe is more commercial than Great Britain, and no nation has waged more frequent wars. Commerce does not prevent war, it merely changes the object of war. Men no longer fight for power or for glory, but for markets and for mines. Napoleon marching to Moscow in order to weld Denmark, Sweden, and Warsaw into a confederation is succeeded by Lord Roberts whose objective is the diamond quarries of Kimberley. Not blockade, but open ports, is the slogan of our modern war. Hence we must look elsewhere for the remedy. Mr. Roosevelt has said in one of the reviews, "The great political revolutions seem to be about complete, and the time of the great social revolutions has arrived." There is only one great social revolution that can ever bring universal peace, and that is the overthrow of egoism, and the supremacy of the Christian faith. "Only the golden rule of Christ can ever bring the golden age of man." The evil demon of war will yield to no exorcism save that of Jesus of Nazareth. When men recognize each other as brothers of the same family, when the spirit of justice and love are universal, then wars will cease, and the trappings of the soldier will become a worn-out delusion and a humiliating memory—relics of the primitive man, dusty curiosities to place in the museum by the side of the stone ax and the witch's ducking stool, to remind the children that the fathers were but little removed from the

> "Dragons of the prime
> That tear each other in their slime."

Nor need the race lose stamina. The strenuous life may be reached without the hardships and self-immolations of militarism. Professor William James has found what he calls the moral equivalent of war: "May not voluntarily accepted poverty be the 'strenuous life' without the need of crushing helpless peoples? We have lost the power even of imagining what the ancient idealization of poverty could have meant: the liberation from material attachments, the unbribed soul, the manlier indifference, the paying our way by what we are or do and not by what we have, the right to fling away our life at any moment irresponsibly—the more athletic trim, in short, the moral fighting shape." Here is something new and something very old. Men may be heroes without brass-buttoned uniforms and fierce battle throes. They may transfer the campaign to their own souls, and by choosing to be poor, or, at any rate, by refusing to "join the general scramble and pant of the money-making street," may prove themselves born of a giant's brood, and may grow a giant's muscles. The meek who have conquered themselves may inherit a conquered earth.

Be that as it may, a new spirit of altruism is abroad in the world, and more than once has it settled an ugly difference. Very fresh is the memory of the demand made by Mr. Cleveland for arbitration in the issue between England and Venezuela. Lord Salisbury at first declared against this method of settlement. It was supposed at the time that this gentleman was driven to a change of policy by the menacing tone of American sentiment. The prime minister who has at call five hundred and eighty-one swift warships is not easily intimidated. It was English sentiment rather than American that brought Lord Salisbury to terms. The English people would overthrow any government that insisted upon an unnecessary war between kindred. The heir to the English throne cabled that he "hoped and believed the question would be peaceably settled." Behind this cablegram was the queen, and behind the queen was the Christian fellowship that binds together the "lords of the strong young land" and the "lords of the sea."

But even the Court of Arbitration has failed thus far. In its last instance it has helped to emphasize the war spirit.[1] In deciding the case against Venezuela it has given preference to those creditors who back their claims by force. It has put a premium upon warships. It suggests that a claimant who bullies is more likely to win consideration, even of a court organized in the interests of peace. The dramatic German emperor stood in Jerusalem and pompously exclaimed, "As was done nearly two thousand years ago, so to-day shall I ring out the cry voicing my ardent hope to all, 'Peace on earth!'" Yet this same complacent pacificator calls the proposed disarmament of

[1] Venezuela *vs.* the European Powers.

Europe "a fantastical idea." "Germany cannot consent to impair her finest instrument of offense; we can stand the expense," he declares. The Czar of all the Russias calls for a world parliament tending toward world arbitration; yet a great war breaks out during a session of this court because of Russia's Machiavelian diplomacy and brutal aggressions, and the president of the council, a subject of the Czar, offers gratuitous insult to an honorable foe.

Until Jesus Christ become the head of the house, armies will go on drilling and navies will go on building. Some day the King who came as Shiloh, who was promised as Prince of Peace, in whose reign the swords were to be beaten into pruning forks, will come to his own. The world is drifting back to Bethlehem. The New England prophetess who "read the fiery gospel writ in burnished rows of steel" has been able to see other signs of the times. Her Battle Hymn kept measure and beat with the tramp of armies and the march of truth. Her white-hot words were sung again and again about "the watch fires of a hundred circling camps." But she has had other visions. It was she who helped to organize the Woman's Peace Association, and it was she who, as a reaction from the *carte* and *tierce* of the Battle Hymn, has written in her old age:

> "Let the crimson flood retreat!
>   Blended in the Arc of Love
> Let the flags of nations meet;
>   Bind the raven, loose the dove.
>
> "Blinding passion is subdued,
>   Men discern their common birth;
> God hath made of kindred blood
>   All the peoples of the earth."

VI

THE PHILANTHROPY OF GOD

VI

The Philanthropy of God

THE God of the twentieth century must be larger than the God of the first century. He has greater responsibilities and a broader field. His duties are immeasurably more complicated and the details of his government more elaborate and more confusing. Once he was the God of heaven and earth and hell, and his relation to these was as simple as their relation to each other. The earth was created first. The heavens were but an adjunct to the earth—a curtain resting upon massive pillars ranged around the edges of the world; and below the earth was the "hollow place" or hell. This was the view taken by the Old Testament writers. This is the heavens and the earth of which the inspired author speaks in Genesis. Indeed, he knew of none other. The sun, moon, and stars that came into view on the fourth day were created because they were necessary to the earth. So they were fixed in the overhanging curtain to give light upon the earth and to rule over the day and the night.

When the earth ceased to be, these heavenly bodies will become useless; and so on that day "the heavens shall pass away with a great noise," the curtain shall be rolled "together as a scroll," and the stars shall drop out "as a falling fig from the fig tree."

There was a marked complacency about all this, and we are prepared for the simplicity of God's dealing with man according to the old records. It is the most natural thing in the world for the Creator to walk in the cool of the day in Eden and hold familiar intercourse with the man and the woman. He had prepared this dwelling place for them, and no other claim could be as imperative as theirs upon his time and attention. The stopping of the sun in the midst of a battle between the clans that struggled for supremacy in Canaan was nothing extraordinary. But little machinery was involved. A brake applied to a single wheel, a few hours' halt of a part of the procession, then the whole incident dismissed with a paragraph.

The universe of God is a modern discovery, and this discovery has revolutionized the world's thinking. The breaking of the earth from its moorings, and its cruise around the sun, has shaken the old theologies. The swift and measureless flight of the sun with its attendant planets about a still greater central body has shattered a whole system of ancient ideas. God's kingdom is now a vast kingdom of suns and constellations and nebulæ. The earth no longer occupies the place of honor. In our new humility we are ready to stand with Rossetti and the Blessed Damosel on the ramparts of heaven which lie

> "Across the flood
> Of ether as a bridge.
> Beneath, the tides of day and night
> With flame and darkness ridge
> The void as low as where the earth
> Spins like a fretful midge."

The God of this new conception must be a larger God. The anthropomorphism of our fathers that pictured him with hands and feet and eyes, that conceived of him as possessed of human passions and weaknesses, cannot abide in this light. He must be reclassified and rethroned.

We need also a kinder God than the God known to our fathers. The world is kinder than it was a hundred years ago and will not be satisfied with the Deity of that date. Man's conception of God is largely a reflection of his own character. "Thou thoughtest that I was altogether such an one as thyself" is the challenge of the Almighty. Jacob the bargainer sought to make a bargain with God. Moses and Israel stooped to pick up the weapons of the dead Egyptians that strewed the shores of the Red Sea; and as the hands that had been accustomed to the trowel laid hold upon the shield, and the fingers that had been warped in the use of the spade laid hold upon the spear, the people were thrilled with new sensations and they sung among themselves, "Jehovah is a man of war, Jehovah is his name." Esarhaddon, king of Assyria, the fighter who conquered Egypt, Arabia, and Zidon, and blockaded Tyre, thus bears testimony to one of his goddesses: "Ishtar, Queen of War and Battle, who loves my piety, stood by my side. Their line of battle in her rage was destroyed. To their army she spake thus: 'An unsparing deity am I.'" Browning in his Caliban upon Setebos has given us the god of the monster. Shakespeare has invented Caliban and Browning has invented his god, following the lines laid down by the master. The god is but a reproduction of the worshiper; the god of the monster is a monstrous god.

> "He is strong and Lord.
> Am strong myself compared to yonder crabs
> That march now from the mountain to the sea;
> Let twenty pass, and stone the twenty-first;
> Loving not, hating not, just choosing so.
> Say the first straggler that boasts purple spots
> Shall join the file, one pincer twisted off:
> Say this bruised fellow shall receive a worm,
> And two worms he whose nippers end in red,
> As it likes me each time, I do: so He."

Caliban was a pretty good Calvinist. He did not dodge the logical consequences of his creed. But men are not monsters. We are living in an age of help and brotherliness. We shelve the treatise on theology which gives two pages to heaven and eighty pages to hell, as Dr. Shedd has done. We repudiate Samuel's dealing with Agag the Amalekite whom he hacked to pieces for the glory of God, or the treachery of Jael the Kenite who murdered Sisera in her tent, just as we abhor the Te Deum of Gregory XIII in honor of Saint Bartholomew, or shudder at the casuistry of the ancient princes of Mexico, who gave notice occasionally that the gods were hungry and therefore they must go to war to secure prisoners on whom these same gods might break their fast.

The question of divine sovereignty is not

as important now as the question of the divine paternity. We are more interested in heaven than in hell; and more concerned about a redeemed and evenly balanced earth than in either. We are looking for large things in God, for we have found humanity to be large and the predication of a Father God makes all men brothers. We have broken with the ancient creeds that localized God. The old formulæ that limited his compassion are shattered. The sun that rises on the evil and the good is God's sun. The rain that falls out of God's skies makes no discrimination between the fields of the just and the unjust. Even our theology has joined the protest of the Quaker poet against the harsh dictum of an ironclad faith:

"I walk with bare hushed feet the ground
  Ye tread with boldness shod,
 I dare not fix with mete and bound
  The love and power of God.

"Ye praise his justice, even such
  His pitying love I deem;
 Ye see a King, I fain would touch
  The robe that has no seam.

"And thou, O Lord, by whom are seen
  Thy creatures as they be,
 Forgive me if too close I lean
  My human heart on thee."

The old ideas of God's awful severity might do for the day when a poor man could be put in jail for a grocer's bill and his wife and children left to starve; when white slaves walked the streets or toiled in the fields with their owner's mark branded upon their forehead; when a friendless fallen woman was compelled to stand in the pillory wearing the infamous scarlet letter "A." When men were harsh they looked for a harsh God. Luther, asked whether the blessed in heaven will not be saddened by seeing their dearest friends tortured in hell, answered: "Not the least in the world." Jonathan Edwards declared that "the view of the misery of the damned will double the ardor of love and gratitude of the saints in heaven." Samuel Hopkins taught that the sight of hell will be most entertaining to those who love God, and will give them the highest pleasure. Amid the uncertainties of this awful faith they sung the hymn which is called "Desperate Resolution," with is implied impeachment of the divine fidelity and compassion:

> "Perhaps he will admit my plea,
>   Perhaps will hear my prayer;
> But if I perish I will pray,
>   And perish only there."

What an alternative is suggested in these words, and how they measure the conception of God! And yet our fathers sung this stanza with earnest zeal, and it is still in the Hymnal!

It is interesting to note the growth of man's conception of the love and largeness of God. He has not always been Love. This is verily his "new best name," and this is peculiar to Christianity. Christian preachers are the only gospel preachers. There is no good news in any other faith. Our forefathers worshiped the most bloodthirsty deities. The earth began in slaughter and ruin. The giant Ymir was produced by the drops of moisture falling into the void from melted ice and snow. He was slain by Odin, and of his blood the seas were made, out of his hair the trees, out of his bones the hills. His skull became the vault of heaven and his scattered brains became the clouds. The world was a vast mausoleum. The horror and shadow of death were upon creation. Thor and his colleagues contend with Fire, run titanic races with Thought, seek to drink dry the sea, and wrestle with Old Age. It is elemental and huge. The gods are drunken revelers and Valhalla is the boisterous taproom of a country tavern. Such gods were feared; they were not loved or respected. Xenophanes accuses Homer of having ascribed to the gods everything that is disgraceful among men. Diogones Laertius relates of Pythagoras that when he descended to the shades below he saw the soul of Hesiod bound to a pillar of brass and gnashing his teeth, and Homer suspended on a tree and surrounded by serpents, as punishment for the things they had said of the gods. These poets but voiced the popular conception. There was no dependence to be placed in the gods, and these interpreters of the age said so. They were the people's poets, and they but spoke for the people.

Then came the deity who was interested in a single race. This was an early phase of theology. It has been a tenet of many faiths. A few nations like the Romans have built their Pantheon and have given a welcome to deities not to the manner born. But in the case of the Roman it was a shrewd stroke of policy to alienate none, to conciliate all; to ostracize only such faiths as the Christian faith, and because it seemed to be the enemy of all. The rule, however, was to elect some deity and to stick to him, or mayhap to hold with persistent consoling confidence that this deity had chosen the people and had for evermore become responsible for them. It was this which gave special horror to the plagues of Egypt. Here was a battle of the gods. Jehovah the god of Israel had crossed into Egypt and had taken the national gods by the throat. Was the Nile worshiped as the Giver of life? This new deity filled it from brink to brink with blood. Look to it, Apis, whose temple is richer than a king's palace, and whose tomb is grand with mausoleum and carven stone. The murrain has invaded thy territory, and even thou art not immune! "Upon their gods also Jehovah executed judgment."

The theory of divine favoritism was Israel's faith from the beginning. Undoubtedly this people were the special wards of Jehovah. He had entered the lists as their champion against all comers. To be sure, they did not at once realize the meaning and the magnitude of this. He was only one among many, and the event must prove whether they were fortunate or unfortunate in the choice of guardian. They still gave place and power to other deities. So when the Ammonite threatened Israel with war because of land robbery Jephthah justified his people by declaring that the land had been given by the national deity: "Wilt thou not possess that which Chemosh thy god giveth thee to possess? So whomsoever Jehovah our God shall drive out from before us, them will we possess" (Judg. 11. 24). It was the *argumentum ad hominem,* and most probably Jephthah spoke as respectfully of the god of their distant kinsmen as he expected them to speak of his.

Slowly did it dawn upon Israel that their God was supreme, and that their position was favored beyond all comparison in having been chosen by such a being. This they realized eventually. But never did they seem to understand the purpose of this election. They were to be a royal priesthood; true, but they were to hold that priesthood for the sake of others. They were to be a peculiar people, but that other peoples might receive the light through them. They were the chosen family of Abraham, but very early in his dealings did Jehovah declare that in them should all families of the earth be blessed. All this, however, was beyond their range. They built the temple at Jerusalem and established bounds beyond which no Gentile dared go on pain of death; they established artificial distinctions of clean and unclean and held it pollution to sit at meat with the outclassed or the stranger. Then they made the sad blunder of thinking that the rules prescribed by God to teach his holiness were intended to emphasize their own sanctity and superiority. So they became a nation of religious aristocrats, imperious and insolent, refusing to bear even the divine message to Nineveh, or to minister to the uncircumcised save at the peremptory command of God.

They crucified Jesus not only because he claimed to be the Son of God, but also because he claimed to be the Saviour of men. Pilate was pleased to inscribe over his head the legend, "King of the Jews," and the priests demanded that it be changed to, "He said he was King of the Jews." But this was not the contention. Because he would not be King of the Jews alone; because he declared that they should come in from the north and the south and sit down with Abraham; because he said, "If I be lifted up I will draw all men unto me"—this is why they crucified him.

Next in order comes the idea that God was especially interested in a single class of individuals. Christianity set out to teach universal love. It was not now a nation, but a race; not now a little province, but a world. The great truth had come. Mankind would soon enter into its heritage. The Jordan of divine love had overflowed its banks and was sweeping over all the thirsty valleys and fertilizing the wide and sterile deserts of human life—"Go ye therefore, and disciple all nations, baptizing them in the name of the Father, and of the Son, and of the Holy Ghost." But again did man blunder. Baptism, given as an initiatory rite, was made an imperative condition. To be sure, every nation and tribe and tongue were to be the recipients, but the church had become the treasury of the covenanted mercies, the guardian of the everlasting love of God, and the church disposed of these things according to fixed rules. There was no salvation independent of the rites of the church. The priest by withholding baptism could withhold heaven. Dante voices the popular belief. On entering the first circle he discovers vast multitudes of men, women, and children. His guide explains:

>   "Ere thou pass
> Farther I would thou know that these of sin
> Were blameless. And if aught they merited,
> It profits not, since baptism was not theirs,
> The portal to thy faith. . . .
>   Some grief assailed
> My heart at hearing this; for well I knew
> Suspended in that limbo many a soul
> Of mighty worth."

"How, then, could he receive baptism?" asks the Princess Danuta in the Knights of the Cross, in reference to Walgierz, who had done only what was acknowledged to be right, and yet who was punished in the next world. "He could not be baptized, and that is exactly why he was sent to hell to endure eternal tortures," answered the monk with authority. Sienkiewicz is writing history. He is giving utterance not only to popular belief, but to formal teaching. The ecclesiastical dictum on this subject is not hard to find. The Council of Trent assembled by the order of Paul III and the sword of Charles V declared, "Whosoever shall affirm that baptism is indifferent, that is, not necessary to salvation, let him be anathema." The French ambassador is said to have protested against the Pope's sending "the Hóly Spirit in a traveling bag from Rome to Trent." The church indicated its will to the council and the council set up bounds to the mercy of God. There was only one kingdom of grace and only one door into the kingdom; and at this door stood the priest with the baptismal ewer in his hand, and entrance was possible by means of this open sesame only. Of any nationality, from any sphere of life, representing any grade of evil, it mattered nothing;

there was room within on compliance with the simple conditions. A few drops of water made the Ethiop white. A shallow form mumbled by a sleepy priest, or flippantly rehearsed by one whose dinner was interrupted and whose mind was upon the fleshpots he had left, and all distinctions were abolished and they that were afar off were brought nigh. But there must be water and there must be this form of words, else God could not reach and save.

Once more there is a move forward. The old religion is reformed, the old creeds regenerated. We now see God breaking down these barriers. His love can no longer be monopolized by a single class, nor retailed by a system of ecclesiastical brokerage. Even as the church proved itself unable to suppress inquiry or to strangle progress, so it proved itself unfit to be the custodian of saving grace. Men found God outside of Rome and died triumphant in spite of withheld sacrament. But alas for human conceptions of the divine! How hardly is it possible for humanity to "reflect as in a glass the glory of the Lord"! Calvinism succeeded Romanism—a distinct advance, but still amazingly and pitifully inadequate: election now instead of baptism; no more distinctions of blood, no more bounds set up by man, no more monopoly of grace; it is now God choosing whom he will love and save, and that irrespective of human conditions or conventional forms. But it is *God choosing!* It is love discriminate. It is, to be sure, a great exultant river of divine benevolence, making the valleys to rejoice and bearing on its bosom the commerce of empires; but it is a river, and a river has banks, and beyond its banks is desert.

On the square in front of the Hotel de Ville, Geneva, they burned Rousseau's Contrat Social, which based all government on the consent of the governed, and which stored the dynamite for the French Revolution. There they burned Emile also, which laid the foundation for Pestalozzi and Froebel and modern elementary education. On an island in the midst of the city they have builded the radical thinker a monument and piled his arms with books. In a dark, gloomy house on a dark, cheerless street there lived in the same Geneva the man who held modern theology by the throat for generations, and whose influence has not yet passed. Rousseau preached the rights of man; Calvin preached the sovereignty of God. Rousseau magnified the human, but he was ahead of his time; Calvin magnified the

The Philanthropy of God

divine, but he misinterpreted it. John Calvin misunderstood the purposes of God, minimized the grace of God, limited the love of God. Yet for all that he was one of the milestones in the way along which journeyed the world to the knowledge of the truth. The world was learning—very slowly, perhaps, but it was learning. God's love is so great, so marvelous, so unexpected that it could not all be grasped at once. Only by these slow processes could the whole truth be apprehended. The sun was rising but there was much of dimness and haze about the dawn. But the day was at hand. Deliverance is to come out of Holland. A gigantic reaction from the harsh theories of Calvin is imminent. Young James Arminius, looking upon the ruins of his native village, and dropping his tears upon the silent face of his mother murdered by the Spaniards, is preparing to grapple with the horrible creed which logically makes God the author of sin. He is not ready to believe that the great heavenly Father has deliberately broken his heart. Called to reply to the layman Koornhert, who has been making dangerous attacks upon the decrees of God, he finds himself in sympathy with the new teaching. From that time until the end he stood for the Love of God. To his mind Jesus Christ died for all men and for every man. God is the Universal Father, and only can a man lose the benefits of salvation by his own choice. This glorious truth, taught in the gospels, preached unto the Gentiles, became the rallying cry of the Wesleys and their associates. This is the outlook to-day. Calvinism has died hard. It captured one branch even of Wesley's fellow workers. It has lurked more or less perceptibly in much of the best thinking of late years. It may still be found in one guise or another in the pulpit and the pew. But it is doomed. We are changing our mental and theological attitude. Not that man is any the less sinful and helpless and undone, but God is more intent to save. Not that law is any the less severe, but love is more pervasive and alert.

We are ready to believe that there is no religious scheme without its gleam of truth. The wildest farrago of superstition, manifesting itself in horrible cruelties, or reeking with sacrifice, has somewhere in its mysterious recesses a right and a reason. God is speaking, and the poor, age-darkened, ignorant soul is struggling to understand and interpret his voice. Side by side on the ceiling of the Sistine Chapel appear the Hebrew prophets and the heathen

The Philanthropy of God

Sibyls, both to represent inspiration. The mighty Angelo preached a mighty truth in the Vatican, a truth which some day will overthrow the Vatican; that is, the catholicity of faith; the nearness of God; the Spirit of God within the spirit of man and claiming all humanity as belonging to him. "Whom therefore ye ignorantly worship, him declare I unto you."

> "God is in all that liberates and lifts,
> In all that humbles, sweetens, and controls."

Wherever men are true and noble; wherever there is a kindly deed or helpful word, there is God. We did not always think so. Some of us, still under the spell of the Genevan logician and creed maker, do not think so now. We thought once upon a time that God attended our church only, or that he lived with those only who knew their Catechism and were sound on theologic questions. We expected all others to be burned in the next world, so we even ventured to burn a few in this world to get them accustomed to the fire. But now we believe that the man, however savage he may be, who loves his little child does so by the grace of God; that the woman, however dissolute she may be, who picks up the stray wet kitten out of the gutter and gives it a saucer of milk by the fire, is listening to the same voice in her heart that spoke to the woman by the well in Samaria, or that greeted Mary on Easter morning.

We do not speak so much about man seeking God as about God seeking man. The Divine Figure standing at the door and knocking is the type of this new school of thought. This is no longer pathetic so much as it is characteristic. The three parables in Luke 15 are bound into one by a thread of gold. The first is not the parable of the lost sheep, though our stately King James has called it so for four centuries; it is the parable of the tender shepherd. The second is not the parable of the lost coin, but the parable of the anxious housekeeper. The third is not the parable of the prodigal son, but the parable of the bereaved Father. It is God's attitude that is emphasized in them all, not the attitude of man. It is the truth as Jesus sees it and as we are learning to see it too. We are harking back to the old dispensation and are remembering that God said as early as the Isaiah prophecies, "I, even I, am he that blotteth out thy transgressions for *mine* own sake."

It is a large day in which we live, and the

sun that makes the light and glory of this new day is the growing apprehension of the marvelous fact that thoughtless though we may be like the wandering sheep, or helpless like the lost coin, or degenerate and unfilial like the younger son, the infinite God changes not his heart toward us, but is bending every energy to succor and to save. The old prophets and seers delighted in painting God with a large, free hand. There was the roll of thunder and the sweep of storm in their descriptions. It was thus they conceived of him, and it was by such lofty conceptions they expected to arouse the interest and strengthen the faith of the people.

"Who hath measured the waters in the hollow of his hand, and meted out heaven with a span, and comprehended the dust of the earth in a measure, and weighed the mountains in scales, and the hills in a balance? . . . Have ye not known? have ye not heard? hath it not been told you from the beginning? have ye not understood from the foundations of the earth? It is he that sitteth upon the circle of the earth, and the inhabitants thereof are as grasshoppers; that stretcheth out the heavens as a curtain, and spreadeth them out as a tent to dwell in. . . . Lift up your eyes on high, and behold who hath created these things, that bringeth out their host by number: he calleth them all by their names."

These were the words with which the prophet sought to comfort the people. This was the "good tidings" that was brought to Zion on account of which Zion was called upon to rejoice. To-day such appeals daze and bewilder us. The universe has grown so large, the boundaries of creation so remote, the heavens that once declared the glory of God are now so crowded with might and mystery, the immensities of space so overshadowing and oppressive, that we are ready to say the God who upholds all this is too large, and his thoughts are not my thoughts and there can be no place for me in his majestic plan. But Jesus the Son of God seemed anxious to meet these very problems. He seemed to know they were coming. "Are not two sparrows sold for a farthing? and not one of them is forgotten before God."

He looks after the grass of the field, the lily that toils not nor spins, and the birds that are without storehouse or barn. He takes time to note the thorns in the flesh; to look into the cruse of oil to see if it is empty. The telescope drags us along through immensities and infinities until with faltering faith we look across an eternity toward a dim, inaccessible God; but the microscope shows us the exquisite gilded feathers on the butterfly's wing, the busy, well-regulated colony that builds its palaces in a drop of water, and we are comforted. The lily of the field knows as much about God as does the planet Jupiter. Yea, the little bird that perches for the night on the swaying twig, under the deep heaven of worlds, is possessed with sweetest content, for the Maker of the ends of the earth has put out his hand over the tiny waif and under his palm does it sleep.

VII

THE SERVICE OF GOD

VII

The Service of God

WE are being told in these later days that our chief business in this world is to grow a soul; not to cultivate farms, nor to build wireless stations, nor to write books; not to formulate creeds, nor to crystallize great truths and preserve them in portable shape for the benefit of the crowd, and so preserve the faith once delivered to the fathers; not even to get ourselves ready for the white robe and the harp of gold: but rather to make ourselves; in patience to acquire a soul; to seek such equipment as shall enable us in the best sense to "serve the present age." Thus Socrates, who was one of the heralds of this century, declares, "I do nothing but go about persuading you all not to take thought for your persons or your properties, but first and chiefly to care about the greatest improvement of your souls." Carlyle writes amid the shadows and limitations of bodily unhealth, "A soul in right health, it is the thing above all others to be prayed for."

Now come the Christian teachers, and they

tell us that this may be reached by the service of God. "If thou return to the Almighty," they say with the Temanite philosopher who had lost his faith in Job, "thou shalt be built up." We speak more or less vaguely of the kingdom of God. It represents collectively the service of God as rendered by individuals. It is according to Harnack "the rule of the holy God in the hearts of individuals, and is a question of God and the soul."

But the kingdom of God is an historic fact. It is not a state of mind, not an imaginary golden age in the past nor a Utopia in the future. There was a time when it did not exist. To be sure, we find germs of it in the old dispensation. The word which was spoken by the Son was aforetime more or less vaguely spoken by the prophets. The passover feast celebrating the death of the lamb and the deliverance of Israel was at its height when the Lamb of God was nailed to the cross. Pentecost, the feast of the harvest, was being observed when the Holy Spirit came upon the disciples and three thousand souls were converted as the first fruits of this new movement. Thus came the kingdom of God into the world like Minerva, armed and self-sufficient, from the brow of Jove; at the same time tracing its lineage back to the old dispensation, in which prophets had spoken and poets had sung and the Spirit of God had fired the hearts of men.

Nor did this scheme begin in myth. It is not a child of the world's midnight. It did not come like Mohammedanism to the desert and lay his hand upon a simple wandering superstitious people. Its voice was not heard first amid the dense forests and dark fiords of the barbaric north as in the case of the old Norse mythology. The world's best centuries greeted its birth. It stood in Athens opposite the Dionysiac Theater, where twenty thousand people sat absorbed in plays that were nothing less than profound philosophical treatises, and that would empty an American theater in half an hour. Rome was in a blaze of intellectual light. Cicero reproduced the speculations of the Greek philosophers. One emperor, Nero, aspired to be a popular poet, another, Marcus Aurelius, is one of the sages whose high, clean thoughts are read by the best people to-day. If Christianity had been a delusion it would have been strangled in its cradle. Its appeal was to well known facts. It said with Paul before Agrippa, "These things were not done in a corner." And so we can walk back in history along a well marked path and can say, "Here, at this time and at this place, Christianity began." We may stand on the hillside at Bethlehem and say, "Here was the beginning, and here the angels came to sing the opening chorus of this world-wide and age-long anthem." We may wander even now in the old Garden beyond Kedron where

> "Into the woods my Master went,
>   Clean forspent, clean forspent.
> Into the woods my Master came,
>   Forspent with love and shame.
> But the olives they were not blind to him;
> The little gray leaves were kind to him;
> The thorn tree had a mind to him
>   When into the woods he came."

We may climb the green hill far away just outside the city gate and with uncovered head and full heart may whisper, "Here on this soil the blood drops fell that were to wash away the sin of the world." Here came forth from this old tomb at the foot of the hill a new morning, and all the universe knew that death was swallowed up in victory.

The kingdom of God is a present fact; not the government of God over the universe. He is King and there is none beside him. But the stars in their courses, and the mountains that melt, and the hail stones and the snow on Hermon are not parts of this kingdom of heaven. It is not God's moral government of man, dealing out justice, visiting transgression with the rod and iniquity with stripes, but showing mercy unto thousands who obey the law. The kingdom means something more. It is summed up in its two laws: "Thou shalt love the Lord thy God with all thy strength," and "Thou shalt love thy neighbor as thyself." Here is an old stone altar down in Mexico in the midst of ashes and charred fragments of bones, and we say the ancient Aztecs were religious and offered sacrifices to the gods. Inside the great pyramid there are proportions and measurements, and we say the early Egyptians were astronomers and read the skies and calculated the times and the seasons. Go into the silversmiths' bazaar at Damascus and climb to the roof, and yonder on the wall of the great mosque may be read in Greek, "Thy kingdom, O Christ, is an everlasting kingdom, and thy dominion endureth throughout all generations." For twelve hundred years this building has been used for Moslem worship; yet these words cut deep in the stone prove that once this building was a Christian temple and this city was a Christian city, though now given up to the enemies of Christ. So these verses about the love of God and love for our neighbor are the shibboleth of this new creed, the great seal of this new kingdom, and they differentiate it from all other faiths that have challenged the confidence of the race.

It cannot be said that these are new words. Love for the neighbor had been commended centuries before the kingdom was born. But who was meant by the neighbor in Leviticus? The man across the street, of the same blood and religion. Whom did Jesus mean? The parable of the Good Samaritan teaches that our neighbor according to this new classification is any man who may need us, any who may be in trouble, any whom he may help, though he be unworthy and disagreeable, and though he live on the other side of the globe.

And this kingdom is to be within us; not in outward deeds, in the march of armies, the building of churches, the raising of money.

"I sent my soul into the invisible,
  Some letter of the after life to spell.
And after many days my soul returned
  And said, 'Behold myself am heaven and hell.'"
                                    Omar Khayyam.

The heart is to be the battle ground and the heart is to be the throne. There the King is to conquer and there he is to reign. So the service of God means a personal relation to God—such knowledge of God as makes us love him, and love him in such degree that we are ready to love those who are made in his image. This is a splendid find. Here is the root of the matter. God is our Father. He is the Universal Father. Therefore Jesus the great Elder Brother will help us to render the largest service. Therefore love for all men will be an important part of this service.

It is this which makes the service sure. This too is important. The old mariner Martin Cockrem, the first Englishman to set foot in the New World, according to Westward Ho, remembered the time when all England thought there was nothing west of Land's End except herring. But now, looking around upon Drake and John Hawkins and Frobisher, he says, "Look to the captains—one's been to the Indies and the Spanish Main and the Russias and the China Seas and round the Cape and around the world of God too, bless his holy name." This is all well enough for restless man looking for new things and planting flags on new islands. But when questions of eternity are at stake we want certainties. The soul resents the interrogation point.

We say, first, that the service of God is a sure service because it has been indorsed by the Book of God. On every page of the book God seems to be giving bond for this life. He says, "This is the way, walk ye in it." He declares that whatsoever is born of God overcometh the world. All manner of figures are used to indicate the absolute certainty of this venture. The righteous shall be as trees planted by the rivers of water, with glossy leaf and purpling fruit; as Mount Zion which cannot be moved. They shall renew their strength and mount up as eagles. A chaotic but radiant flood of confused but splendid rhetoric to show the wisdom of righteousness and the security of the righteous. These are the words of a Book which claims to be able to make us wise unto salvation. This is the chart that marks out the safe places. Here speaks a voice which assumes to be supremest authority.

But how is the Book indorsed? If the Bible goes security for God who will go security for the Bible? The Romanist meets that question with ease. He has an infallible Pope and council. The Protestant does not so easily surrender his right to think. So with him the Bible must be proved as other books are proved. It was reason which decided in the fourth century how many and what books should be in the canon, and it is reason which to-day when properly safeguarded must give its indorsement to the holy volume. When Copernicus declared that the earth moved about the sun and swung in a great orbit through the stars it was not at once accepted. The earth itself journeying down the heavens established the contention of the great astronomer. Sir John Mandeville wrote a book seventy years before Columbus was born in which he declared that "The lond and the See ben of rownde schapp and forme, . . . and men myghte go be Schippe alle aboute the World, and aboven and benethen." Yet for scores of years sailors were afraid to steer too far into the west for fear they would reach the edge and so fall off. Only the tremendous facts in the case, the discovery of America, the mighty stretch of sea room as ships pushed out into the Pacific, and on around the Cape of Good Hope and back with eager haste into the familiar Atlantic—only this gave the seal of authority to the strange words of the ancient traveler.

The Bible must be its own advocate and witness. We have revised our apologetics in the later years. The old arguments are out of date. Bishop Butler in his redoubtable Analogy staked the integrity of the Bible upon miracles. Christianity, he claims, was first received upon the allegation of miracles, and is thus distinguished from all other faiths. Paley argues from design in nature, and thus proves the existence and wisdom of God. But the world has grown since these knight-errants went forth to war. We have lost our definition of the word "miracle." The boundaries of the supernatural have been pushed back, almost annihilated, indeed. We are doing every day that which would have been a miracle in the days of Chrysostom or Peter the Hermit. We are losing the sense of wonder. No one knows what will be possible to-morrow. We no longer prove the deity of Jesus by his miracles. Given his deity, we expect the miracles to follow. They become deductions rather than credentials.

The broadening of the universe has outlawed the argument from design. We are more modest than our fathers were as to the final causes. Perhaps the sun was created to give us light, but we are not so sure of it since we have become acquainted with the family of planets, each of which depends upon the sun, and have also learned that the sun is but one of millions moving on their mysterious errands down the skies. We have modified our views of efficient cause as well. God is not only the great First Cause of the theological schools, but he is an ever-present Power manifest in every effect. Paley's famous watch did yeoman's service in its day and generation, but it is on the shelf now, and it will run no more. The Bible deals in statements of fact. It concerns itself with everyday life. It is susceptible of proof or disproof every hour of the day. Said Professor Huxley, "For three centuries this book has been woven into the life of all that is best and noblest in English history." Coleridge writes, "The Bible reaches me in lower depths of my soul than any other book." Is the book true? Ask the man who goes into sin. Tell him that the Bible says that "the wicked are like the troubled sea when it cannot rest, whose waters cast up mire and dirt." Is this not a picture of his soul? Ask the man who turns away from sin. Tell him that the book says, "The ransomed of the Lord shall come with songs and everlasting joy upon their heads, and they shall obtain joy and gladness." And he will answer, "These are inspired words, for they are the words of the soul."

There is on every luminous page appeal to human consciousness. In the spirit's deep and solemn chambers the Christian believer has met and talked with God. This vision of the invisible, this apprehension of the unknown, comes in a sudden bewildering burst of light and power to some; to others it comes as the morning comes. Nobody can say at this moment, "It is night," and the next moment, "It is morning." At the same time, when the morning has fully come and the golden day stands squarely and gloriously across the eastern skies and reaches its hands to the farthest horizon, nobody doubts that the night is gone. Talk to the exulting Christian of the uncertainties of the Christian faith! Tell him that in the very nature of the case there can be no apprehension of supernatural things —that the idea of God is so vague and ambiguous that there can be no definiteness in religious experience! Ask the radiant world when the birds are singing, and the mists are rising from the valleys, and the yellow glory of the morning is crowning the tall pines along the mountain side, if it knows that the sun has risen. Ask the orchards that are beginning to feel the thrill of new life in every fiber, the robins that are busy all day long looking over last year's nests and scolding to each other from tree top to tree top over the damages wrought by the winter's storms; ask the grass along the curbstone—ask all these if they know that spring is at hand. Ask the frightened, sobbing child who wakes up alone in the night and cries out in distress, if it knows the mother's voice that answers it through the dark, and the mother's face against which a moment later it lays its baby cheek; then ask the Christian whose heart is in the keeping of the Most High how he knows there is a God, and how he knows that this God is interested in him.

All this is testimony to the written Word. It is the language of the Spirit as crystallized in the Book that has become the language of experience. In fact, there has been no definite religious experience that does not in some way connect itself with the Bible. "Compare the statements given respecting the power of the gospel by Jonathan Edwards, by a converted Greenlander, a Sandwich Islander, and a Hottentot, and you will find in them all a substantial identity. And their statements respecting these things have the more force because they are not given as testimony, but seem rather like notes, varying, indeed, in fullness and power, which may yet be recognized as coming from a similar instrument touched by a single hand."

The service of God is certain because Christianity has a living Head. Hugh Price Hughes has strikingly developed this thought. Jesus has met all the world reformers on their own ground and has shown his superiority. There is much in which they resemble him. There comes a time when the greatest of them fails. He was a Teacher, we say. So confessed the unconvinced Nicodemus; only a Teacher sent from God could do his great works. But so was Mohammed, the cameldriver of Arabia, and so was Confucius, the reformer of China. Jesus was a wonderful Example. Holy, harmless, undefiled, separate from sinners, his life sheds a clear white light upon the centuries. So also was Buddha, the light of Asia; so also was Zoroaster. Their lives were clean, their hearts were pure, their example was exalted. Jesus died for others. So did Socrates die that his countrymen might have the inspiration of his integrity. So did John Brown. This grizzled visionary, this fanatical but fearless revolutionist, set out single-handed to defy the civil and military power of the United States and to throttle the evil of slavery, and died in the end for the sake of human liberty.

Thus far have other teachers and reformers walked side by side with the Nazarene Jesus. But now they part company. When we say that Jesus of Nazareth arose from the dead and sitteth at the right hand of God, the living Head of the new church he founded, we have crossed an eternity, and human helpers and human saviours are lost far down the horizon, hopelessly out of the race. Christianity is not an opinion as to the best way to keep the moral law and to get the most out of life; not the history of a man who lived twenty centuries ago and of the church that has perpetuated his teaching. Christianity is life—the life of Jesus Christ, who is himself Life, in the heart of the believer. Of course it is certain: he is here to testify to its truth. Of course it is certain: he is here to walk with his followers in the hard ways. Of course it is certain: he is here to open wide the door into eternal habitations.

Perhaps there is a better meaning in the old question, "What shall it profit a man, if he shall gain the whole world, and lose his own soul?" This verse has passed into the stock phrases of the strolling evangelist. It suggests the strain and intensity of the high pressure revival service, or the drum and tambourine of the Salvation Army barracks. We are learning nowadays that the man who saves his soul is the man who lives the largest and fullest life. There is meaning in every cloud that comes out of the west, in every leaf that turns toward the sun, in every wave that whispers along the beach, and it is the soul in man that interprets this meaning and thrills with a sense of its beauty. Nature cannot keep a secret from one who has a right to know. She does not try. She lives with open window when he is about. She instructs every plant and bird and summer stream to take him into their confidence. The horse sees only the grass of the meadow and knows that it is good to eat. The man with a soul sees the clover blossoms and hears the dreamy hum of the bees and catches the distant clear note of the meadow lark or the bobwhite, and the meadow becomes a poem. The child who seeks to build a better house of his blocks, the schoolboy who tries to make a straighter mark in his notebook, the student who turns another leaf of his Homer and sits up a little later so that his recitation will be better than it was yesterday, these show the working of a soul.

This has exalted nations. It has built cities, and enacted laws, and fostered civilizations. The savage who wanted to make his stick more effective as a weapon sharpened the end. Then he found a bit of pointed flint and he used that as a barb. Later, when he had iron, this was used in place of flint. Since as he has developed he has invented the bow, the firelock, then the rifle, all the while following an ideal and seeking to realize it. The beaver builds the same sort of dam he built in the rivers of paradise; the cell of the honeybee in the market yonder is in no sense different from that which Samson found in the carcass of the lion among the Syrian hills. But man knows there are better ways. He longs for better things. He sees the top of the mountain, and frets that he is as yet far down the slopes. He dreams of the ladder which Jacob saw, and he knows no reason why he as well as the angels may not ascend that ladder; indeed, he will not be satisfied until he has tried. Salvation is twofold. We are to be saved from and we are to be saved to

—saved from sin and littleness and atrophy, and saved to the fullest and richest life; saved, as said in the Prologue, in the Old Testament sense by elimination, and saved in the New Testament sense of reconstruction and evolution.

We are in danger of loss as never before. It is a world of brick and mortar and wheels. The sun has no time to paint a thousand rainbows in the morning dewdrops, nor to linger in golden splendor before he drops the crimson curtains of the evening: his business is to set the time for the factory whistle. The sparkling little stream from the hillside ripples down to the city, for here it expects to find men and women who will sit down on its banks and children who will wade in its happy waters. But it is throttled by an ugly dam, jostled into the slimy mill race, and sent staggering along to turn the great wheel, for there is no place in this bustling world for the dilettante and the trifler. What can we do? What time has the man who knows nothing but his business, who thinks about it all day and dreams about it at night, what time has he to see visions? The most beautiful thing in all the world to him is the smoke that smells of trade. The bank where the wild thyme grows possesses no attraction comparable with the bank where he makes his deposits. Promissory notes for him, bird notes for dreamers. The workman who spends his hours in the confusion of shops and amid the clash of cogwheels, the woman who drudges in the back attic—what time have these for the cultivation of the soul?

And yet for all open, eager hearts there is opportunity. Robert Burns following his plow on the April morning throws the sod over a meadow daisy, and the "wee modest crimson-tipped" flower becomes a part of the world's treasures. He uproots the nest of a field mouse and "the best laid schemes of mice and men" becomes a part of the world's literature. Longfellow found a revelation in the village blacksmith's shop; Bryant saw poetry in the planting of the apple tree; Kipling found inspiration in the rush and roar of the battleship Iowa. There is food for the soul if we are looking for it. A single high thought, a longing desire for better things, a verse of Scripture, will open new fields, will show us the beauty and the glory in the commonplace, will feed the soul and make it grow in spite of the struggle and strangle of our sordid days.

How, then, will it profit a man if he gain the whole world and lose his power to appropriate and to appreciate? What we receive from life depends not so much upon our environment as upon our capacity, our soul power. The world belongs to the man who can receive it. All the beauty and all the glory of life come to his door and say, "We are yours if you can take us." Here are the long crowded shelves of the library—a great new populous world; yet how many there are who pass by and only remember after they are gone the peevish complaint of the Old Testament cynic, that of making books there is no end. Here is the picture gallery. These masterpieces do not belong to me. They have cost their owner vast sums. But if I am able to hold communion with the high souls who put on the marvelous coloring, the pictures belong more certainly to me than to the man whose money bought them and who estimates them by the dollars' worth. When God made the world beautiful he had in mind those among us who can appreciate beauty, and every orange tint of sunrise and every amber glow of sunset was put there for their benefit. They are God's wards and they are nature's favorites

"Who through long days of labor,
 And nights devoid of ease,
Still hear in their souls the music
 Of wonderful melodies."

Walk forth, ye chosen ones, pure in heart, simple in life, kindly in deed. All things are yours, and ye are Christ's, and Christ is God's.

VIII

THE LAW OF SERVICE

VIII

The Law of Service

AT the beginning and at the end of his life did Jesus the Jew receive homage from the Gentiles. The Magi came from the east to kneel at his cradle, the Greeks came from the west to gather round his cross. The last act of his public ministry, before he entered upon the dread passion week, was to give audience to the Greeks who came to Philip saying, "Sir, we would see Jesus." It is possible that the visit of these strangers was of political significance; that, indeed, the Greeks were looking for a national deliverer; that while the Magians came bringing gold, frankincense, and myrrh, the delegation that sought an interview on this particular day came to offer Jesus a crown.

There is nothing incongruous in this. Jesus of Nazareth was certainly a prominent figure. In the eyes of the politics of the day he was a coming man. His strange power over his fellow men was conspicuous. It was not forgotten that centuries before there had been veiled, half ambiguous utterances in reference to just such a man as he was proving himself to be; that the government should be upon his shoulders; that in his name should the Gentiles trust. Startling were the developments in Judea, and, more startling yet, Judea did not seem to appreciate the situation. The man who was winning the admiration of the world was suspected and ostracized at home. While all eyes were turned hopefully toward him his own people were unfriendly and had even planned his overthrow. This was the world's opportunity; and we can readily understand how such an errand as this would suggest itself to the alert Greek mind.

Moreover, it would be in perfect harmony with the history of this elect people. At each crisis of their national life there had arisen a national deliverer. History had again and again crystallized about an individual. It was a hero-loving race, and there had always been heroes when the necessity arose. The Trojan War dragged on its dreary length with Achilles sulking in his tent. By and by he was placated, then Jupiter said to the assembled gods, according to Homer:

"Troy must soon be overthrown,
If uncontrolled Achilles fights alone.
Assist them, gods, or Ilium's sacred wall
May fall this day, though fate forbids the fall."

THE LAW OF SERVICE 179

The great cloud of Persian invaders had found a Miltiades waiting at Marathon, and a Leonidas in ambush at Thermopylæ. Now Macedonia had overrun the peninsula and Rome had succeeded Macedonia, and the great burning question was, "Who will deliver us from Rome?" So came this delegation to the celebrated Galilean, to offer him perhaps a kingdom and a sword and the opportunity to write his name in blood upon the pages of history side by side with the military giants whose memory was the nation's pride. Then said Jesus, "The hour is come that the Son of man should be glorified." "You have read aright the signs of the times. This is as you suspect the crisis (κρίσις) of the world; we are on the threshold of a gigantic revolution. But you have very naturally misconceived the spirit of the hour and the agencies of the revolution. It is not by life, but by death; not by conquest, but by self-surrender. The weapon before which shall go down the turbulences and the tyrannies is not an unsheathed sword, but an uplifted cross. The world is to be led to the feet not of a monarch crowned with far-flashing gems, but a friendless, despised, fugitive peasant crowned with thorns."

Here was a new system of political economy. This was an astonishing view of the political situation, and showed that this man who was now being interviewed was strangely ignorant of human affairs, or that he had made some marvelous discoveries not yet revealed to the race. What a straightforward Reformer was Jesus Christ! How little he cared for public sentiment or the majority rule or questions of expediency! What a tremendous sensation he would create to-day; how cordially he would be hated and how industriously would the party bosses and the society leaders sneer at his utopianism! Straight through a subject did he penetrate, and without any reference to immediate results he launched his theories upon the world.

Nobody was ready for the bewildering thesis announced in this interview. We have no means of knowing what these Greeks thought of the man whose counsel they had sought, or of the platform he had outlined. The historian is suggestively silent, but Paul speaking generally said, "Christ crucified was to the Greeks foolishness." It was not in the beaten track, not according to the methods of the fathers; it did not seem the best way to secure the most votes and to maintain the balance of power. What use had they for a dead man? They were arranging for a triumphal procession, not for a funeral. They had more confidence in a scepter than in a tomb. They had monuments enough in their own classic land, and what good were they? What they wanted now was a throne and a man seated upon it who could reach one hand to the bounds of the east and the other to the bounds of the west and bring back the ancient glory of this proud and cultured race.

But stay a moment, disappointed and silent ambassadors; have there not already been foreglintings of this unique and revolutionary idea? A modern poet dares to put in the mouth of Prometheus, who challenged Zeus to "hurl his blanching lightnings down," these strange words—strange because spoken in the fret and fury of the awful struggle between the king of the gods and the unconquerable Titan:

"True power has never been born of brutish
    strength,
Nor sweet Truth suckled at the shaggy dugs
Of that old she-wolf. Are thy thunderbolts,
That quell the darkness for a space, so strong
As the prevailing patience of meek Light,
Who with the invincible tenderness of peace
Wins it to be a portion of herself?"

We would be ready to cry out against the idea that "the invincible tenderness of peace" could be regarded as a winning force in these old days of muscle and of might. But Lowell has not made a slip. Other watchers in the night had caught a glimpse of the morning. Even stern and rugged Æschylus causes this same world-giant, Prometheus, to say:

> "Do ye also ask
> What crime it is for which he tortures me?
> That shall be clear before you. When at first
> He filled his father's throne, he instantly
> Made various gifts of glory to the gods,
> And dealt the empire out. Alone of men
> Of miserable men he took no count,
> But yearned to sweep their track off from the world,
> And plant a newer race there. Not a god
> Resisted such desire except myself.
> I dared it, I drew mortals back to light.
> For which wrong I am bent down in these pangs
> Dreadful to suffer."

Lowell has been reading Æschylus. He has discovered a deep, solemn undercurrent in the thought of this early and boisterous age. He finds a fragment of the gospel of peace and of sacrifice in the work of this colossal genius who learned his life lessons as a soldier at Marathon and as a sailor at Salamis, and who marshals gods and demigods and mountains

The Law of Service

and seas and eddying lightnings upon his sky-roofed stage. The Delphian oracle which declared at the beginning of the Persian War that either Sparta or one of her kings must fall kept Leonidas at Thermopylæ when outflanked by the foe. He, the king of Sparta, would die and thus save Sparta. By the crisp shores of the northern ocean the same truth is taught. Thor, the god of thunder, the son of the supreme god and mediator between the gods and man, wrestles with the Midgard serpent which as the symbol of evil lies coiled around the world; beats him to the earth and slays him. But Thor gives up his life in the struggle.

And surely this is no new idea to the Jewish mind. In the midst of the splendid rhapsody of Zion Redeemed, beginning with the fortieth chapter of Isaiah, a strange mysterious winning figure is introduced—the Servant of Jehovah who is commissioned to carry out the purposes of God in the world. And through the wonderful chapters that follow, this figure moves, fairly eclipsing Jehovah in his majesty and importance. All the world is acquainted with the Servant. His patience, his gentleness, his mission to the helpless and the lonely, his courage; his sad face set like a flint against his persecutors, yet without form and comeliness. This has been written on human hearts and has molded human lives. Whatever the unknown prophet might have meant originally, it is now almost universally conceded that these words apply to the Messiah. And so in this great Book of the olden time there are strangely contradictory statements. The coming Deliverer is to be called Wonderful, Counselor, the Mighty God, the Father of Eternity, the Prince of Peace; and at the same time he is to be "despised and rejected of men; a man of sorrows, and acquainted with grief." No wonder the national mind was confused and there was expectation more or less definite of two Messiahs. The first would be the son of Ephraim or Joseph, and he would be slain in the war of Gog and Magog. The other would be the son of David and he would bring the war to a successful issue, restore supremacy to Israel, and cause all nations to walk in his light.

The American patriots who signed the Declaration of Independence were setting a price upon their heads. But an old school history used to say that every signature was made in a firm, steady hand except that of Stephen Hopkins, who had the palsy. John

The Law of Service

Hancock's large, bold characters were made, we are told, so that George III might be able to read the name without spectacles. The climax of heroism and self-surrender was reached when Charles Carroll took the pen. For fear there might be uncertainty because the name was a familiar one, he wrote it all out—"Charles Carroll of Carrollton;" as much as to say, "Here I am, gentlemen; I am the man and am ready to take the consequences of my action." The old story of the Pompeian Guard belongs to the same gospel of self-sacrifice. Vesuvius hurled its avalanche of fire over the doomed city. The unofficial, irresponsible multitude surged past him frenzied with fear, dizzy with the heave and shudder of the earth. But he was on duty; he was a Roman soldier; and there he stood in the whirlwind of death, and there his body was found in the ripening of the centuries to show how a man can die for a cause which seems worthy of his death.

Here and there, written and unwritten, in ancient and modern times, among civilized peoples or in the midst of savagery, have been hints and suggestions. The God-thought was speaking at sundry times and in divers manners to the fathers. Only by slow process and through years of training did the real truth come home. In the Church of the Capuchins at Rome is Guido Reni's Archangel and the Devil, symbolic of the triumph of right over wrong. The attitude of the angel is graceful and studied and correct. Not a fold of his garments is disturbed, not a lock of his flowing hair is astray. He is trampling upon his terrible enemy as he would pose at a social function or enjoy a four-o'clock tea. And so says Hawthorne's Miriam, who had struggled and who knew the awful meaning of wrong: "The Archangel, how fair he looks with his unruffled wings, his unhacked sword, and clad in his bright armor and that exquisitely fitting sky-blue tunic cut in the latest paradisaical mode! With what half-scornful delicacy he sets his prettily sandaled foot on the head of his prostrate foe! No, no, I could have told Guido better. A full third of the Archangel's feathers should have been torn from his wings. His sword should be broken halfway up to the hilt, his armor crushed, his robes rent, his breast gory! The battle was never such child's play as Guido's dapper Archangel seems to have found it." Miriam is right; Guido is wrong. The picture is false. It does not stir the blood. Let us festoon it with honeysuckle and forget-me-nots, and hang it in my lady's bower. A recent picture by Riviere of Saint George and the Dragon preaches a truer gospel. The great scaly coils of the monster are wound tight about the dying horse. The hero himself has fallen faint and breathless, while the anxious-faced princess bends over his prostrate form. This tells the story of struggle; of right face to face with wrong, and suffering in order that wrong may be conquered; of sacrifice as the price of salvation; of remission by the shedding of blood.

The religious instincts and aspirations of the world have been full of this great doctrine. The human race, from the day it was scattered bewildered and homeless at Babel, has been groping its way to Calvary. All the sacrifices that have ever been offered upon the world's altars, from the lamb in Israel to the writhing victim under the knife of the Druid priest, or the hapless woman lashed upon a high platform at Benin to be devoured by vultures, all these have been guideboards for the world's following. Some one must risk or give up or suffer for the common good. And when Jesus the wonder worker, the man who trod the waves and stilled the storm and raised the dead, gave himself into the hands of his enemies and became obedient to death, even the death of the cross, men said after the first bewilderment, "It is just what we have been waiting for, just what our poets have been singing, and our prophets have been promising, and our hearts have been hoping." The Cross becomes the key to all the black problems of human failure and human woe, and the man who is lifted out above the earth is the one Man who is able to understand and to help all other men.

This principle is scientific as well as theological. It is written in God's larger volume. It finds "tongues in trees, books in the running brooks." Look abroad through nature and is not this the parable—that life comes only through death, that to-day is born in the tomb of yesterday, that every quivering stalk of wheat is a monument standing over the grave of a dead grain? Yonder goes a great ship plowing through the waves and spreading its white wings in the sunlight like some gigantic butterfly; and such it is, for many a noble tree has gone into the chrysalis state in the shipyard, to come out by and by this thing of beauty and embodiment of grace. The prolific vegetation of the Carboniferous age lived its teeming life and then died, and lo, centuries later it appears as coal, the motive power of the great good natured but capricious dragon that thunders along the iron track; or cozily crackling in the grate it tells the story of its prehistoric birth. Death has always been at the birth of life. Its shadow has always been the first to fall across the cradle. Sacrifice has been the bridge over which passage is made from the old to the new. Out of the stones that have closed the door of ancient sepulchers have been builded the cathedrals that stand for modern faith.

In the same year there came from the press two books that were destined to mold opinion with strong, masterful hand—Social Evolution, by Benjamin Kidd, and The Ascent of Man, by Henry Drummond. Both were written from the standpoint of Christianity, and are essentially reverent in their tone; yet the difference between them is organic. Mr. Kidd sees only the struggle for existence, the blind, selfish "grapple of life with its environment." Anything of unselfishness, of altruism, of morality that may be found in the race is a contribution from without, the introduction of new conditions, the intrusion of a new force or factor into human life and history. Self-denial, he teaches, has no root in nature, no analogy in the brute creation, and we must look for its philosophy as for its origin in that which is extraneous to man. He insists that any deepening and softening of character, at any time manifest, is the direct and peculiar product of the religious system. His definition of religion as concerned with social phenomena is, "Religion is a form of belief, providing an ultrarational sanction for that large class of conduct in the individual where his interests and the interests of the social organism are antagonistic, and by which the former are rendered subordinate to the latter in the general interests of the evolution which the race is undergoing." It may be said that this represents the scientific and the theological view up to very recent date.

Mr. Drummond announces a much larger creed. He has caught a glimpse of a great truth or a great error. His book thrills with a new and grander gospel of facts. He is not the discoverer. Alfred Russell Wallace hinted it when he said that there came a time when "variations of intelligence became more profitable to the primates than variations in body." John Fiske elaborated this idea and gilded it

THE LAW OF SERVICE

with his luminous imagination. But Henry Drummond sent it forth to the world dressed in everyday clothes and speaking in everyday language. He claims that the old-time evolutionist has read but one table of the law; has listened only to the curses from the Mount Ebal of science. Over against the thunder-scarred peak of Ebal is Gerizim, and the voice that speaks from this summit is the voice of blessing.

Side by side with the struggle for life so splendidly elaborated by Charles Darwin is the struggle for the life of others which Mr. Darwin did not see; a voice which he did not hear, yet a voice which has in it the love songs of the ages, the altruisms, the patriotisms, the crucifixions of all the sweet-voiced centuries in which men have been climbing toward the light. And this is the parable of nature. Down to the minutest germ cell this principle of sacrifice holds. In order that this cell may reproduce it must disintegrate. If it would perpetuate the life contained it must give up a part of itself. The flower dies that the seed may mature, the seed dies that a new life may be created. The starch or albumen stored by the plant about the mysterious life atom becomes the food of man. We are feeding every day upon the product of self-sacrifice, of unselfish forethought. We take for ourselves that for which the plant died in order that it might bequeath it to its children. Every tree in the orchard, every grain stalk in the cornfield, every tall weed by the roadside is living for others, and is ready to die for others. The doctrine of self-sacrifice comes to us fragrant with the odor of ten thousand blossoms and rich with the yellow fruitage of ten thousand harvest fields. Self-preservation is no longer the first law of nature. There is no self in nature. Pope's sarcastic arraignment of human pride becomes the watchword of this new scientific gospel:

"For me kind Nature wakes her genial power,
 Suckles each herb, and spreads out every flower:
 Annual for me, the grape, the rose renew,
 The juice nectareous, and the balmy dew.
 For me the mine a thousand treasures brings,
 For me health gushes from a thousand springs;
 Seas roll to waft me, suns to light me rise;
 My footstool earth, my canopy the skies."

This is not self-love, but a large reading of the new gospel writ all over the world. This is the meaning of the cross, that great overshadowing mystery of the ages. Jesus the Nazarene was here illustrating the very crisis

THE LAW OF SERVICE 193

of this Otherism, this self-forgetting self-surrender which has been hinted at in literature, in art, in religion, and in nature. The Man who hung upon the cross was humanity, was cosmic being, at its climax. We shade our eyes when we catch a glimpse of his radiant figure enveloped by the cloud on the Mount of Transfiguration; we are thrilled with awe as we see him walk forth from the sepulcher when an angel was his page and an earthquake was his herald; but Jesus the King of kings and Lord of lords on the cross with thorn-pierced brow and nail-torn hands was nothing less than God manifest in the flesh, whose death was the crowning glory of his life, the highest exaltation of love, the supremest fulfillment of law.

It means the survival of the humane. It has taught us not only to scorn but to hate the formal curses of the church, such as were launched at the Dutch Republic. It brings recoil of horror at the advice of Amherst to Bouquet to inoculate the Indians with smallpox in order that they might be destroyed by wholesale. It fills us with revolt when Napoleon orders his gunners to fire round shot upon the ice of the lakes at Austerlitz upon which six thousand Russian fugitives had huddled for safety, until the whole mass sunk into the chilling waters. And it prepares us for the better days and the larger sympathies, in response to which Washington can say at Yorktown to his exultant soldiers, "Don't cheer, my men, posterity will do that for us;" and Commodore Philip can say on the battle-swept deck of the Texas as the Spanish flag goes down, "Don't cheer, boys, the poor devils are dying."

"The victor looks over the shot-churned wave,
  At the riven ship of his foeman brave,
    And the men in their lifeblood lying:
  And the joy of conquest leaves his eyes,
  The lust of fame and battle dies,
    And he says, 'Don't cheer; they're dying.'

"Cycles have passed since Bayard the brave—
  Passed since Sydney the water gave,
    On Zutphen's red sod lying:
  But the knightly echo has lingered far—
  It rang in the words of the Yankee tar
    When he said, 'Don't cheer; they're dying.'

"Why leap our hearts at that captain's name,
  Or his who battled his way to fame,
    Our flag in the far East flying?
  The nation's spirit these deeds reveal—
  But none the less does that spirit peal
    In the words, 'Don't cheer; they're dying.' "

IX

THE GOSPEL OF A PERSON

IX

The Gospel of a Person

In the midst of the Orations of Moses which make up the greater part of the fifth book of the Bible is the Book of the Covenant. In the midst of the Book of the Covenant is a striking prophecy. The author or editor is discussing the national life of Israel. This he treats as affected by three persons or offices: the King, the Priest, and the Prophet. These three give visibility to the divine rule, stability to religion, and insure progress in social and individual morals. The duties and the limitations of the King are first set forth: chosen of God from among the brethren, simple in tastes, loyal to the truth, a keeper of the law himself and so an example and an inspiration to his subjects. The Priest is next considered, and sundry warnings and injunctions are spoken for his direction. Then in reference to the last office we read the familiar words: "The Lord thy God will raise up unto thee a Prophet from the midst of thee, of thy brethren like unto me; unto him shall ye hearken."

The reference is most likely to the prophetic order rather than to any individual prophet. Moses is noting the relation of the people to God. They are to have kings, but only such as shall be of their own blood and of the Lord's appointing. They are to have priests in order that religious worship shall be sustained and religious form perpetuated. And finally, as an offset to the enchanters and necromancers of the strange land they are to possess, there is to be a line of prophets who will be able to prove their genuineness by certain fixed tests, and who will be able also to satisfy the cravings of the human heart for the supernatural. There would be as ever a hungering after God and the unknown. This hunger, responsible as it was for the magicians and sorcerers of Canaan, would be met by the true prophets of God.

This is the most natural interpretation of these words. At the same time the interpretation given by Peter, and the reference of this prophecy to Jesus Christ, is in accord with the methods of inspiration. The local need for communication with God which should find a local supply but represents the universal need, and this larger need was to be met by the Messiah. This is Old Testament usage. The very word Messiah was applied to the High Priest of the day in anticipation of the great High Priest who should be "holy, harmless, undefiled, separate from sinners." Other instances of a dual prophecy occur. In the midst of the decline and fall of Israel, Hosea appeals to early history to prove the eternal care of God:

> "When Israel was a child, then I loved him,
> And called my son out of Egypt."

These words are seized by Matthew, ever eager for an Old Testament corroboration, as applying to the asylum given by Egypt to the infant Jesus. The purpose of Hosea was a simple one; Matthew, however, makes his words a link in the chain of prophecies that attest the Messiahship of the Nazarene. The Old Testament prophet was looking backward to the beginnings of Israel; the evangelist under the influence of the Holy Spirit reads a remarkable forecast in these apparently obvious and artless words, thus connecting the bondage of Israel in Egypt forever with the history of the world's Redeemer.

There is taught here in this remote past a prominent feature of modern theology—the gospel of a Person. The people at the time of this promise were in dire straits. They had never seen higher hills than the Mokkattam hills that overlook Cairo. Now for months all about them had towered the notched, lightning-blasted peaks of Sinai. They had known only the voiceless deities of Egypt, here the rocks had quivered before the words of this new God. In dismay they had cried out, "Let me not hear again the voice of the Lord my God, neither let me see this great fire any more, that I die not." Then it was that Moses promised a far-off better dispensation and a Prophet who should live among men and whose teaching should make hard things easy and rough places smooth.

This is the modern need—a personal Saviour; the redemption of men by a Man. The world cannot be saved by doctrine. It has never been without a generous supply of these, and they have not been without their use. Men have sought to frame in words their conceptions of God and of life, and we have called these formulæ doctrines. We have no right to say that there is no utility and no power in these conceptions. God is the God of the brain as well as of the heart. He can help in our opinions as well as in our emotions and our activities. If we have reason to believe that he will assist in the performance of duty we may also look for his assistance in the conception of duty. He is perhaps as willing to make for us our theology as to regulate our ethics. As the Saviour of the world possibly he is not unwilling that we understand some of the processes of salvation.

There is heard in some quarters an outcry against theology. The unfortunate science is between two fires. It is attacked from the side of rationalism, and it is also severely buffeted from the opposite camp of a rigid evangelism. On the one hand, those who are learned and proud of their learning have outgrown theology—for which they are profoundly thankful; on the other hand, those who are ignorant and proud of their ignorance have no place for it —for which they offer praise. It is to the former a fossil; a trussed and crumpling mummy; a bit of amber in which, like a luckless fly, are imprisoned the ideas of the past. It is only a curiosity now reserved for the showcase of the museum. It does not count in the sum of modern forces. It has no place in the modern pulpit. The railroad strike, the problem of the wage earner, the ethics of the wedding ring—these are current, and theology has gone into limbo with astrology and the maelstrom and the sea serpent and other strange and uncanny superstitions of an early day.

The opposite school has no use for doctrines. Its disciples tell us that the gospel is and ought to be the theme of the preacher; though what they mean by the gospel as distinct from a definition of the gospel they do not deign to explain. However, according to their notions theological seminaries are intended to be incubators where the ministerial bird is hatched and thence sent out properly catalogued and labeled; with his claws duly pared to keep him from scratching in the smug and rectilinear landscape gardening of the fathers, and his wings prudently clipped to keep him from flying into his neighbor's yard.

All this is narrow, and one school is as narrow as the other. If we have truth it is surely no crime to attempt the definition of that truth. On the other hand, it is no surrender of our faith, nor an impeachment of the fathers, to insist upon the liberty of changing our definition whenever our standpoint changes, or of adding to that definition should a larger segment of the truth be apprehended. We must have a creed. Do they say, "Creeds are rigid"? Yes, as rigid as the rails that run over

The Gospel of a Person

hill and valley, spiked down so that the swift express may thunder from one end of the continent to the other. But allowance is made for expansion and contraction on the most rigid lines. Do we say, "Creeds are narrow"? So is the line of safety on the chart, marked by the buoys and along which the ship must be brought if it would escape the rocks. But a wiser pilot with better tools may discover a better channel, and we do not sail long with the doctrinaire captain who keeps to the old course because it is marked on the old charts. The prodigal son had a creed. He realized its breadth and force when among the swine. The dying thief had one. It came to him in awful power as he hung on the cross side by side with the man who was to him the Lord of life and death. The tiniest child who folds his hands and says, "Our Father who art in heaven," has uttered a whole body of theology, enough to thrill the heart of an angel or to save a race of men. And yet it is not a doctrine that the world wants most. In itself it is only a definition, and definitions belong to the dictionary, not to the heart. It is only the prescription and suggests the method of cure.

Nor is the world deliverance to be effected by a morality. There has never been a lack of moral precepts. Christianity has no monopoly of truth. All truth is not in the Bible. The Bible did not make the truth. It was the truth which made the Bible, and it was too large to get all of itself into one book. The Indian poet who wrote of God,

> "If with the heart you seek him
> He's here, he's there, he's everywhere;
> Go where you will you meet him,"

had not been reading our Bible. God had spoken to him by some other voice. The world had much of the Sermon on the Mount before it was preached. Very little of it is really new. David and Isaiah had caught a glimpse of the hilltop on which Jesus sat as he uttered these magnificent words. Jesus as the Messiah of the New Testament was but quoting in certain phrases what he had said before as Jehovah of the Old Testament, or what had been said by his servants. That which had been scattered through thirty centuries was now crowded into half an hour. The flowers that had bloomed along the hillsides of the world's history were gathered and compressed and distilled, and the result was a drop of the attar of roses which we call the Sermon on the Mount,

Indeed, we may find fragments of this sermon in the Encheiridion of Epictetus, and in the philosophy of Marcus Aurelius. Here, by the way, was morality enough for the world's following. But the smooth platitudes of the Greek philosopher and the chaste periods of the Roman emperor have never very seriously affected human thinking or living, while the Sermon on the Mount has conquered the world.

The power which is to transform the race is not abstract, but concrete. It is not subscription to a creed, nor obedience to a law, nor indorsement of a system of morals. It is devotion to a Person. "For I know *whom* I have believed" is the first Apostles' Creed. And herein lies the secret of victory: a Person, real, live, substantial, potential, the exponent of truth, the substance of law, the personification of love; a "who" instead of a "what"; a Man instead of a method; a being who is himself all that we ought to be, and all that we long to be. This is the need of modern theology, and this need is met in Jesus Christ.

Now, what manner of Person is this to be? Had any conception of the true need of the race dawned upon the mind of this old-time seer? Can it be that centuries ago when the world was young, before the race had in any large sense come to a knowledge of itself, before Homer had showed the might of human passions, or Job had uncovered the deeps of human sorrow, or Shakespeare had swept his master hand over all the chords of the soul, that even then the children of men knew what they would wait for when the days of knowledge had come? This old-time prophecy is a matter of to-day. It is as fresh and as current as the morning paper. It is girding its loins, and taking its staff in hand, for it has business with the twentieth century. It is truth, and "the eternal years of God are hers."

The Prophet is to be like Moses, and Moses was a deliverer. The instincts of deliverance dominated him from the beginning. He killed the Egyptian whom he saw smiting an Israelite. This was not murder; it was rescue. He befriended the daughters of Jethro, and chivalrously gave them the right of way at the wellside in Midian. The surprised young women hastened to say to their father, "An Egyptian delivered us out of the hand of the shepherds, and also drew water for us." They were mistaken as to his nationality, but not as to his mission. He did not wait to introduce himself. It was perfectly natural for him to be helping somebody. He was a gentleman of the old school. He was always on the side of the weak. He seemed born to make things better.

And deliverance is still needed. The Egyptian taskmaster is still in the land. The shepherd daughters of the people still suffer at the hands of the strong and heartless. The Midgard serpent still lies coiled about the world, and the race is waiting for Thor, the youngest of the gods. We have not yet outgrown the idea and the fact of sin. We may not call it by the names our fathers used. We may not trace it to the same source, nor seek to apply the same remedies; but we are conscious of its presence and shudder as they did at its power. When we would do good, evil is present with us. It is on our streets, it is in our homes, it is in our hearts. It is not a theological dogma, but a fact. We do not learn of its existence in the Catechism, but in the cradle. We do not take it as a part of our intellectual furnishing, a theory the acceptance of which qualifies us for ecclesiastical recognition; but as part of our world knowledge, knowledge that forces itself upon our notice as soon as we touch life.

And it is the same old heartbreaking, home-wrecking agency that it has always been. Men may come and men may go, but it goes on forever; leaving the serpent trail that blighted the blossoms of Eden and cursed the generous earth; driving its Juggernaut car down the crowded thoroughfares of the latest century just as it swept down the first or the eighth or the twelfth.

> "Never a king but had some king above,
> And never a law to right the wrongs of love,
> And ever a fangèd snake beneath a dove,
>   Saw I on earth."

The world has had a Deliverer for centuries, but the world is not yet delivered, and there is still work for Moses or for one like unto him. This delivering Christ, whose form appears on the raging currents of our modern life, whose voice sounds along the halls of trade and invention, was promised long before there was any modern life. We may call his deliverance by any name we please; load it down with mediæval scholasticism, or blur it with modern affectation, or disguise it with the euphuisms of science, it is still deliverance from sin, and it is the deliverance the world wants and must have.

Moses was a leader of his people. Out of

Egypt meant the wilderness. He who delivered them from the fleshpots must lead them through the desert. His work had but begun when they shouldered the weapons that had drifted to the shores of the Red Sea, and raised the song of thanksgiving. We are again in the wilderness. Our world is a world of doubt. This is especially an age of inquiry. The interrogation point is on our coat of arms. The advance of physical science has jarred so many of our traditional beliefs. Dana and Lyell and Sedgewick have modified our ideas of creation, and have shown us wrinkles on the fair face of the earth which prove her much older than we had inferred from the ancient and approved interpretation of Genesis. Galileo and Kepler and Young have revealed to us the size of the universe, and have indicated how big an undertaking it was for Joshua to stop the sun in mid course; and some have even dared to wonder if even the conquest of Canaan was worth the trouble and confusion of such an experiment. Traditional theology has been driven to explanation and concession. Many of the settled convictions of the fathers have been unsettled, many of our shibboleths have become obsolete, and the fountains of the great deep have been broken up. Once losing their childhood faith, many have gone on from doubt to despair. "It cannot be denied," writes Mr. Disraeli, "that the aspect of the world to those who have faith in the spiritual nature of man is at this time dark and distressful. What is styled Materialism is in the ascendant. This disturbance in the mind of the nations has been occasioned by two causes: first, by the powerful assaults on the divinity of the Semitic literature by the Germans; and, secondly, by recent discoveries in science which are hastily supposed to be inconsistent with our long-received convictions as to the relation between Creator and created." A popular novelist declares that he who seeks for truth must "wander alone into the land of Absolute Negation and Denial. In this land it is always night and the earth is covered with ashes."

It is a pathless wilderness which lies beyond Egypt. We must have our Moses even to-day. It is the Way and the Truth and the Life that is needed as never before. We are waiting for the man who knows—one who has touched life at both extremes; who was before and who is after; who has noted the path from the beginning and who has explored it to the end. Browning in his high-ranged Brahmanism has said;

"Sorrow is hard to bear, and doubt is slow to clear.
Each sufferer says his say, his scheme of the weal
    and the woe.
But God has a few whom he whispers in the ear,
    The rest may reason and welcome."

God is not exclusive. He is ready to whisper to any man who is ready to listen. We have met in the streets of our cities, under the dome of our churches, in the home of luxury and in the home of want, the Divine Man who is whispering in the ear of all the sorrow-broken and suffering; who is leading the race through the desert to Sinai and Horeb; who will inspire the heart even of those who fall by the way with the thought that they are pilgrims toward the light and that their lowly graves shall mark out a sure path to the land of promise.

What a colossus was this Moses! We are just beginning to learn the breadth of his personality, the range and sweep of his brain. He was centuries ahead of his age, while skilled in all the learning of that age. Though of the slave caste, he found his place in the highest circle of Egyptian life when Egypt meant the climax of civilization. The latter-day jurist goes back to these old laws enacted in the desert as the basis of modern jurisprudence.

The physician acknowledges that the health regulations of the camp of Israel antedate the sanitation of this clean and favored century. The philanthropist longs for the day when men shall deal with each other after the manner prescribed in these ancient documents. The statesman recognizes in Moses the founder of a commonwealth in which was the germ of the modern republic. Whatever the people needed they found in Moses. Did they ask an example in self-sacrifice? Here was a man who as the adopted son of Thermuthis sat at the king's table and commanded the king's armies. Yet for the sake of his brethren in bondage he refused to be called the son of Pharaoh's daughter, "choosing rather to suffer affliction with the people of God than to enjoy the pleasures of sin for a season"; esteeming the reproach of Christ—that is, the reproach which Christ suffered in the oppression of his people, and which Moses suffered with him—as greater riches than the treasures of Egypt. Did they ask an example of moral courage? Moses set out alone for Midian to defy one nation and to deliver another. Then with a full knowledge of desert life and a keen realization of its hazard he led the helpless thousands away from the cornfields of the Nile valley. He might in some respects have lived in any age. He might have been a contemporary of Lycurgus, and perhaps he could have softened the rigid laws of this man of iron without taking the nerve out of them. Easily might he have stood with the Gracchi when they went forth to redeem Rome, and his voice and his wisdom might have saved this national reform and saved the reformers as well. When Ambrose met in debate the eloquent Symmachus and won the Roman Senate to Christianity, the tact and the statesmanship of Moses would have saved the church from many of its excesses and sent it pure and clean down the future. This cosmopolitan genius would have been at home in San Marco with Savonarola, could have trodden with Bradford and Standish and Carver the deck of the Mayflower, or have sat at Lincoln's elbow when he signed the Emancipation Proclamation.

A Prophet like unto me! How clearly does this far-visioned seer realize that just such a leader is necessary—a man who will be neighbor to every man; whose range is not affected by time nor posited by race peculiarity; one whose words and whose spirit will be heard and understood in every age and in every clime and in every social stratum. The great painters have given us pictures of the Christ, and these conceptions have been tinged by the environment and the personality of the artist. Da Vinci, for instance, shows us the tender Christ; Titian shows us the human Christ; Angelo represents the conquering Christ; Raphael gives the divine Christ; Correggio and Guido Reni paint the suffering Christ; and Hoffman brings us the Christ beautiful. Even the sacred writers, as suggested elsewhere, give us different phases of the same character. No two could see alike. Matthew sees in Jesus the fulfillment of the old-time prophecies, the completion and the climax of the Old Testament dispensation. Mark portrays the Conqueror. His verbs are in the present tense. He hurries from event to event, from victory to victory, in one great sweep of power. Luke sits down quietly at his desk to give us as a student the life of a Man. As historian he records the details of his parentage and childhood. As physician he is minute in his treatment of clinical cases; as artist he gives us dainty studies of life scenes and incidents. John is one of the Sons of Thunder. He sees the Eternal Word, dwelling in the shadows with God; the Almighty Creator of all that is, made flesh and dwelling among us; concealing yet revealing the glory of the Father; giving life; promising the Spirit; discipling the world.

But, after all, none of this is adequate. Jesus of Nazareth cannot be taken at a single sitting. He is not a Jew, nor a Roman; he is not Aryan, nor Semitic; not Italian, nor English. He is the one man who is never an anachronism, and nowhere an alien. His words are still damp from the press. We wake up in the morning and find his spirit in the leading editorials, we listen to the sound of hammers out our back windows building the hospital after his plans. The smokeless powder leaves the atmosphere clear so that we may see his cross upon the battlefield; and with the red cross go the newest scientific instruments and the latest appliances for comfort and help.

> "I know not what the future hath
>   Of marvel or surprise,
> Assured alone that life or death
>   His mercy underlies.
>
> "I know not where his islands lift
>   Their fronded palms in air;
> I only know I cannot drift
>   Beyond his love and care."

X

JESUS AND THE NEW AGE

X

Jesus and the New Age

JESUS CHRIST always faces the new century. There has never been a day when this could not be said. He is every man's contemporary. He is part of every age. Strong men have so stamped themselves upon historic periods that these periods have been called after their names. So we have the Gregorian age, the age of Charlemagne, or of Thomas à Becket, the Augustan age, the Napoleonic, or the Bismarckian. These men have seemed to be suited to the day in which they lived. They would not be at home elsewhere. Abraham would be out of place in the present century. Cromwell would be an anachronism in the England of Edward VII. Martin Luther would create but little sensation by nailing his protest upon the door of our modern church. Rare is it to find a man whom the world has never outgrown; who keeps pace with its swiftest progress. But such is the Divine Man to whom the world more and more bears witness. He is just as manifestly in the world now, and just as definitely a part of current history, as when he paid the taxes in the province of Galilee, or answered the charge of treason before the Roman judge.

Moreover, he is the one Person whom the world has never been without. Before the enrollment on the census of his supposed parents in Bethlehem and the register in the temple of the birth of a son in the royal family, he had walked with men and watched the progress of events. We talk sometimes of dispensations—the Patriarchal, the Mosaic, the Levitical, the Christian, etc.—but this is superficial. There is but one dispensation. There has been but one plan of salvation and but one Saviour. This plan has never been changed because of new conditions and unexpected contingencies. God has never been taken by surprise. He has never remodeled his campaign. With stately, resistless tread his purposes have marched on to their fulfillment. There has been but one true religion, even as there has been but one astronomy. There may be a Ptolemaic system with a few great truths and many speculations, and a Copernican system that moves in a mightier sphere and touches remoter horizons, and a nebular hypothesis whose factors are gigantic constellations and on whose dial plate an eternity is registered; but it is all one astronomy. The same sun has always driven away the winter and the dark, and the same stars have walked serenely across the sky.

The world has always had this one true religion, in part or in its fullness, in prophecy or in fulfillment, in the word spoken by the angels, or in the great salvation spoken by the Lord. And Jesus Christ has always been the prominent figure of this eternal scheme. His associates in the flesh need only "search the Scriptures," the Old Testament Scriptures, and they will find there abundant and emphatic testimonials to himself. The two disciples walking to Emmaus, bewildered by the awful events of the crucifixion week and the sudden downfall of their hopes, listen to the expounding of all the Scriptures, "beginning at Moses and all the prophets," and lo! they are full of the things concerning Christ. The Ethiopian eunuch reads the words of a prophet, words written centuries before, and when from Philip he hears the story of the crucified Jesus, the sublime being who inspires the prophetic pen and the humble Nazarene are seen to be the same, and he craves baptism in this confidence. Here is a book that records the world's beginning and that is dark and awful with portents of its end; a book that has grown with the growth of the race and has noted in graphic lines every step of the upward path; a Book whose pages have been written in waste and weary deserts, in palaces of cedar, in homesick captivities amid alien splendors, or by the seabeach of lonely islands; written by kings and poets and shepherds and fishermen; but through it all from cover to cover walks one supreme Personality, by whom it seems inspired and of whom it seems a biography.

And this one Man has adapted himself to every age. He is always and everywhere close to life. He is always able to meet the local need. In the world's first stages, when men were few and manners simple, he walks in the garden in the cool of the day. He talks familiarly with the man and the woman. He is so human and so natural that they shrink abashed at his presence only because they have learned that they are naked and not because he is God. So we find the representatives of the different eras giving voice to their confidence in and recording their experience with Jesus, the great Jehovah of the old dispensation. Abraham binding upon the sacrificial altar his son Isaac, the son in whom all his hopes for the future are centered, and trusting with a blind, passionate trust that God will help, sees the ram caught in the thicket and cries out, "Jehovah-jireh"—"The Lord sees our need and will provide." And greatly did the patriarch and his family need a Provider, for they were in the midst of a strange land with strange customs, and the future was full of untried problems. Moses stood on the hilltop with Aaron and Hur, and Amalek fought with Israel. And Moses held up his hands in prayer, and Aaron and Hur supported him on either side. So Amalek was discomfited and fled away down the dark mountain passes. Then Moses built his altar and called it "Jehovah-nissi"—"Jehovah is my banner"— for sorely did the people need a victorious leader, a mighty standard as a rallying point. The wilderness was before them. Amalek was only the first of the desert tribes that should lie in wait for them in their long and awful journey. But the battle cry was to be, "The hand on the banner of Jehovah: the war of the Lord against Amalek." And with this conquering watchword they should march straight through the wilderness.

Again in Canaan the Angel came and sat

under an oak and watched Gideon threshing the little grain he had concealed from the Midianites. The land was overrun with the enemy, and Israel was without a leader or an army. Then the Angel said to Gideon, "Surely I will be with thee, and thou shalt smite the Midianites as one man." And Gideon called the altar he built then and there "Jehovah-shalom"—"The Lord is peace." For Israel longed for peace, that the people might plow their acres and trim their vines. Then in the days of Jeremiah, when Israel was being smitten by the hosts of Babylon, when national ruin seemed imminent, the prophet looked for a day and looked for a deliverer and said his name shall be "Jehovah-tsidkenu"—"Jehovah our righteousness," the Lord who by righteousness was to bring back prosperity to the elect people. This same idea is magnificently illustrated by Ezekiel, the vision seer, the brooding mystic of the ancient dispensation. By the rivers of Babylon he reads upon the sky the history of the captive people. He looks and the glory of the Lord departs from Jerusalem and stands upon the mountain on the east side of the city, and the city is left desolate. Then in the process of time Israel repents; the temple is builded and measured, and then the glory of the Lord comes from the east, and his "Voice was like the noise of many waters, and the earth shined with his glory." It was the supreme vision of the cherubim and the fire and the wheels that had beforetime gone out. And in the rapture of his joy the prophet, in a burst of eloquence that rivals the apocalyptic rhapsodies of Saint John, shouted that the name of the city from that day should be "Jehovah-shammah"—"The Lord is there."

And so this Jehovah-Jesus moves like a conqueror through the Old Testament records. He is everywhere present and everywhere the center around which move the hopes and the aspirations of the race. When he steps into the New Testament the same profound effect is produced—he is every man's friend. He is abreast of every question. He is consulted in reference to matters domestic, social, and political. His assistance is sought in the division of inheritance among legal heirs; his opinion asked as to the comparative claims of Gerizim and Jerusalem as shrines of worship; his intercession sought even in the presence of death. The people, indeed, recognizing that he is the ideal man, the man for the times, clamor to make him king.

Pass on to the apostolic times. Jesus is gone. The shock is so recent that there has been no time for reaction. The young church is stricken at the heart. There is no assurance of permanence. Indeed, there is every reason to believe that the present economy is passing. The foretold "tribulation" is at hand. The eagles are gathering together from the ends of the earth for the rending of the carcass. The wild disorders in the city of Jerusalem and the fierce fanaticism of the various religious sects are preparing the way for Vespasian and Titus and national ruin. And now the Jesus of the day is the Jesus of the Second Advent. Every word he had spoken in reference to his return is treasured up. Every day the heavens are scanned to find the heralds of his approach. Did he not say that he would come "immediately after the tribulation of those days"? and the awful days are passing and the Son of man is due at any moment. Had he not sent a message to the Asiatic churches in which he announced, "Behold, I come quickly: hold that fast which thou hast"? And so Paul was but voicing the sentiment of the day when in nervous but glad anticipation he wrote, "The Lord himself shall descend from heaven with a shout, with the voice of the archangel, and with the trump of God: and the dead in Christ shall rise first: then we which are alive and remain shall be caught up together with them in the clouds." This stalwart representative of the faith expected to stand at his post until relieved in person by the Master. In the maze of national disorder, the overwhelm of human institutions, the wreck of states, it was the Christ who steadied and strengthened his followers. His star was already on the eastern horizon; his figure was preparing to step out upon the sea whirl, and all would again be peace.

Later along, when the field broadened and when the church seemed to be a permanent institution, or at any rate when it seemed necessary that it be permanent, then Jesus appeared as the Founder of the church. All that he had said in exaltation of religious organization was remembered and emphasized. It was noted that he had pledged his church to stand against all the assaults of the gates of hell. It was kept fresh in mind that by his own word whatever the church bound on earth should be bound in heaven; that disputes should be settled by the church; that matrimony should be contracted only within the limits of the church. To the Crusaders Jesus was a man of war. In the days of Angelo, when the world was governed by force, he appears in the great picture of the Last Judgment as a powerful giant who by his resistless arm sweeps sinners into the pit of destruction. The age seemed to need a muscular judge able to execute his own sentences, and they found it in Jesus the Son of God.

To-day we are in the midst of social problems. It is the age of industrialism. Questions of labor and capital, of the rich and the poor, of city government and of the family—these are crowding about us. There is a realization that the age is out of harmony. There is a sense of inequality, a "consciousness of contradiction between economic progress and spiritual ideals." The disturbance is radical. Not the scholar alone in his dressing gown and slippers, but the grimy-handed workman, the weary woman who watches out the night, all are studying the problem of life and its unequal burdens. There is also a subtle confidence that this age is to settle these questions. And so the reformers are at work; from the red republican whose slogan is "Property is robbery," to the prophets of brotherhood and even justice like Dr. van Dyke, who says:

"This is the Gospel of Labor,
  Ring it, ye bells of the kirk:
The Lord of Love came down from above
  To live with the men who work."

Now, has Jesus Christ kept up with the swing of thought? Is he an outworn tradition, or unwearied and fresh does he still walk abreast of the century? There is but one answer to this question. His is the word that is supreme to-day. In their newest finds, in their broadest philanthropies, in their ripest and purest politics, men say they are only "going back to Christ." No, not going back to him. It is a new discovery of the old truth that the world has never lost him, never outstripped him, never passed beyond his range and reach. Not "back to Christ," for lo, he is at our side, emerging with us from the mistakes and selfishness of the past generations, the explanation of such emergence, and the inspiration of the new age with its new and marvelous problems. So writes Edwin Markham of what he conceives to be a new discovery:

"Balder the beautiful has come again;
Apollo has unveiled his sunbeamed head.
The stones of Thebes and Memphis will find voice:
Osiris comes; O Tribes of Time, rejoice!

And social Architects who build the state,
Serving the Dream at citadel and gate,
Will hail him coming through the labor hum;
And glad quick cries will go from man to man,
'Lo, he has come, our Christ the Artisan;
The King who loved the lilies, he has come.' "

Not by communism is this industrial problem to be solved. This is beating a retreat. This is going back into the kindergarten. There can be no individuality in such a scheme, nothing but the blight of an unreasoning and sometimes unreasonable uniformity. Society is not to be saved by individual self-effacement. Even the communism of the early church did not take away personal initiative. "Whiles it remained, did it not remain thine own? and after it was sold, was it not in thy power?" is Peter's challenge to Ananias, who sinned not in withholding a portion of his possessions, but in professing to bring all. Nor is the reform to be effected by philanthropy. The suffering classes are not asking for mercy, but for justice; not for sympathy, but for standing; not that their needs be supplied, but that their conditions be changed. To give alms to a man who demands a hearing and has a right to expect it; to organize bureaus of charity and soup-kitchens when the cry is for arbitration, is to insult the spirit of the age, and to postpone for only a breathing space the day of reckoning.

And so in the passionate suicidal conflict between labor and capital Jesus Christ brings his message to capital, that character is more than wealth, that treasure is to be laid up in heaven. He has a message of fidelity to labor, "Be faithful in the little things and by and by you will dwell among the large things; serve well and you may be served." In reference to the employer he teaches that "unto every one that hath shall be given"; that is, a man has a right to expect returns from his capital and his skill. To the employed he teaches that all men should have living wages, for "the laborer is worthy of his hire." And unto both he shows himself to be the great servant of all. "The Son of man came not to be ministered unto;" not to rule, but to serve.

And even the modern phenomenon of industrial opportunism finds a prophecy in his words. The laborer of to-day is the capitalist of to-morrow. But this is not only a new opportunity, but also a new responsibility. The new master must remember the days of his apprenticeship the new employer deal squarely with his old associates. This is the teaching of Jesus. The man of the parable by whose fidelity and skill the one pound became ten pounds was made ruler of ten cities. The reward for duty well performed was added responsibility. There was no discharge from service, no retirement from business, no escape from obligation. In proportion to his success was his new burden; he who dealt in pounds was to care for cities; he who handles tools and who succeeds is to become responsible for the well-being of men, women, and children.

The kingdom of God. This was the burden of his message. This was the promise of his forerunner, who said, "The kingdom of heaven is at hand." This was the subject of his first sermon. This was the mission of the seventy, who were sent out "to preach the gospel of the kingdom." This is the substance of his parables. This is the first plea of the great prayer he taught: "Thy kingdom come." The kingdom of God! The kingdom of God! He spoke of it and preached it and died to establish it, and now we are calling it "the brotherhood of man," or "the gospel of humanity," or "altruism," or what not; but it is the same great social ideal which came out of Bethlehem and was forever sanctified at the cross, and which in these later days is coming down to us bringing God's solution of all our human problems, and God's cure for all our social ills.

Never has there been such pressure upon the integrity of the family. Europe, Canada, and Australia granted 20,000 divorces in 1889; there were 23,000 during that year in the United States alone. The ratio of marriage to divorce in Massachusetts went down from 45 to 1, to 31 to 1, in twenty years. The family is seriously threatened by the growth of individualism. It is held that the unit of ancient society, the family, is to be superseded by the unit of modern society, which is the individual. Thus declares Sir Henry Maine; the civil law taking account more and more of the individual. This is the tendency more or less marked of modern religion. Protestantism has been criticised as "an extravagant form of individualism." "All our modern notions and speculations have taken on a bent toward individualism," is the verdict of Horace Bushnell. Added to this is the entrance of women into industrial relations on an equality with man. This also tends toward the dissolution of the family group. How can there be a home, we are asked, with its sanctity and with its traditions, when man and wife spend all the time in the office or in the mill? These are the tendencies, on the one hand. On the other hand, socialism would merge the family into the state. "Domestic unity is inconsistent with an absolute social unity vested in the state. The family institution is an evolution; it was necessary in the elementary conditions of society; it is now outgrown and must pass away in the interest of a larger and fuller growth. The continuity of society will no longer depend upon the private nursery."

Jesus has a timely word for this new danger to society. With him the family is supreme. He dares to correct Moses, who had permitted a man to put away his wife. This was a compromise. It was an expedient of the kindergarten. The day of such compromise is past, and now a man shall leave his father and his mother and cleave unto his wife, for so it was in the beginning. In this he again shows himself abreast of the age. Science has but recently explained the origin and shown us the evolution of the family. In burning words we have been told how motherhood has grown to be the glory of woman, and the redemption of the race; how through long ages of struggle and sacrifice the modern family has been born. And Jesus is now remembered to have said centuries ago, what he is again saying to this century, that this family institution, toward which nature has struggled, this social order which we are almost ready to accept as accidental, and which we are told must be abolished in the interest of a larger evolution, is the divine ideal; that all mankind is, after all, but a great family, and that God is the universal Father. "Family affection in some form is the almost indispensable root of Christianity," is the latest utterance of Social Science." The twain shall become one flesh; and what God hath joined together let no man put asunder," is the old-time declaration of Jesus, and it proves that in this respect also he knew what would be the needs of the race.

Men are holding Peace Congresses and are pleading for arbitration, but there is nothing new in this. The angels told the world of that many centuries ago, and said that the Bethlehem infant was born to bring "peace on earth to men of good will." We hear much of the newest discovery in theology in reference to the Fatherhood of God and the brotherhood of man, and we are told that William Ellery Channing and Horace Bushnell and Henry Ward Beecher made this discovery. Why, the world has been calling God "Our Father" for countless generations on the authority of the great Elder Brother, and so his old teaching is the newest, freshest thought of this fresh and vigorous age. In fact, better than ever before do we realize that the Christianity of Jesus is a force within the individual, and that this force finds expression in the effects produced by the individual. If there is evil this force is seen in its effort to remove the evil. If reform is necessary the world can depend upon the man in whom is the spirit of Christ. Is some measure necessary to lift up the fallen or to ameliorate the condition of those whose lives are barren and hard, then "by this shall all men know that ye are my disciples, if ye have love one to another," is the word that levels differences and sends a man on his ministry of mercy.

XI

THE EVOLUTION OF THE BOOK

XI

The Evolution of the Book

THE Bible is not a book, it is a library. It is not a birth, it is an evolution. It is not Athena who sprang fully armed from the brain of Jove; it is rather Dionysus, who, sewed up in the thigh of the thunder god, grew steadily to his intended proportions. Its first chapter and its last are centuries apart. No man who saw its beginning saw its ending. The world that received the Revelation was vastly different from the world that greeted the Pentateuch. The author of its earlier pages had no conception of the startling retinue that should tread in his footsteps and supplement his work. The *dénouement* of this great world drama was hidden in the mind of the world's Creator for centuries after the prologue had been spoken.

There is indeed a marvelous plan, and it moves toward a marvelous climax; and when we consider the conditions under which it was announced we are impressed with the magnitude of the enterprise. The Scriptures themselves do not hesitate to acknowledge a plural origin: "God having of old time spoken unto the fathers in the prophets, by divers portions and in divers manners"—"fragmentarily and multifariously," as this phrase has been freely construed; each revelation a fragment of the one great truth, and each incomplete of itself. The Koran, if we are to believe tradition, was written by Gabriel in the seventh heaven, on silk, and dictated to Mohammed in the first heaven. The prophet there inscribed it upon parchment and mutton bones, and deposited it in a chest. It all came in the lifetime of Mohammed.

Sixteen centuries pass from the time that Moses wrote until the last epistle was penned. We say from the time that Moses wrote, for, whatever be the result of the battle royal of the critics over the authorship of the Hexateuch, it is quite certain that some of it will be left to Moses; while, indeed, there are portions that are of still more ancient date, according to the critics. The world as we know it was young when the first pages of the Book were written. Luxor and Karnak were new. The mighty Hittites dominated Syria, and all the north from Magog to the Greek isles, with headquarters at Kadesh and Carchemish.

Egypt was splendid with pyramid and temple, and, freed from the hateful regime of the Asiatic Hyksos kings, had changed her habits of seclusion; had assembled her armies at Megiddo and had "washed her heart," as the old inscriptions say—that is, had avenged the national insult and had humbled her age-long enemy. Assyria had emerged from its vassalage to Chaldea, and the hosts were gathering along the Tigris that in the process of time should shake the walls of Jerusalem.

While Moses was in command of Israel he wrote portions of the Hexateuch. This seems to be implied by the text. How much or how little he wrote we do not know. The book of Genesis is made up largely of separate documents. How many of these documents there are, and just what is their arrangement, has not yet been decided by the scholars, but the Priest's Code, the Yahwistic, the Elohistic, and the Deuteronomic are familiar to the student of the Bible, and must be reckoned with. This portion of the Scriptures did not reach its completed form until the days of Ezra and Nehemiah. The book of Judges was perhaps written in the time of David, as an historical summary of the steps that led to national unity. Ruth was written at the same time in order to give the ancestry of the reigning king. Many of the Psalms were prepared at that period for public service. Then came Solomon, during whose reign many of the Proverbs were put into shape, and probably Job was written. And so on down through the nation's growth and eventual decadence. At intervals the voice sounded and the world was richer for history or prophecy or song.

Then came the New Testament message when all the roads of human history led to one Rome, and when Rome, whose hands touched the horizon, was kneeling at every shrine and listening to every oracle in the hope of hearing words that live. The old Sibylline books had been destroyed with the temple of Jupiter. The new collection made by the Senate and revised by the higher critics under Augustus did not satisfy anxious souls. Then out of the East came the truth. In uncouth Greek it was clothed; the literary artists said it was as the chattering of the rook, but the library was complete, and the world is reading it, and has found it able to make wise unto salvation.

Even those portions of the book which are contemporaneous are strikingly dissimilar in style and finish. The brand of mind as well as the fluctuation of time is set upon its pages. Its writers did not lose their individuality, and are very sharply differentiated even when of the same race and period, and illuminated by the same manifestation of the Spirit. No better illustration of this can be found than in the case of the four evangelists. They are writing the same story, recording the same life, yet each has his own purpose and each stamps his own personality upon his work. The gospel of Mark, which is thought to have kept closer to the primitive material than any of the others, is anecdotal in its character. There is a briskness about it, a crisp, alert expedition, that has led the critics to call it "the gospel of the present." The motto of the author seems to be the word "straightway." This he uses on all occasions, and it gives a nervous alacrity to his style which the others do not exhibit. Matthew is didactic. He deals in the sermons and discourses of Jesus. His purpose seems to be to show that Jesus is the Son of David, and he is fond of linking the actions of the Nazarene back to some event or prophecy of the olden time. "That it might be fulfilled" is the brand of the first gospel. Luke shows Jesus as a reformer; and John dreams mighty dreams of his deity. But in all there "worketh the one and the same Spirit, dividing unto each one severally as he will."

What could be more strikingly different than the involved parenthetical style of the Epistle to the Romans, the studied logical sequences of the Epistle to the Hebrews, and the transparent simplicity of the Epistles of John? Where can we find greater antithesis than exists between the practical matter-of-fact James and the dark, mysterious, unfathomable Apocalypse? The poet did not cease to be a poet when he became the mouthpiece of Jehovah. He still saw the glory of God in the heavens. Deep still called unto deep, and the morning stars still sang together. Matthew the publican is interested in the episode of the tribute money, and records how the stater required for taxes was found in the mouth of the fish. Luke the physician uses the language of Galen and Hippocrates in describing diseases (Luke 4. 38, 39; 16. 20). The other synoptists use the colloquial word $ραφίς$ for needle in the proverb of the camel and the needle's eye; the doctor among the evangelists uses naturally $βελόνη$, which means a surgeon's needle.

Moreover, the Bible was not written as one book. As late as Chrysostom it was called

The Evolution of the Book 245

"the books." At that time it had not been bound in one volume. When Paul wrote his letter to the Colossians he wrote one to the Laodiceans also. He then directs that the Laodicean epistle be read in the church at Colosse, and the Colossian letter be read in Laodicea (Col. 4. 16). Evidently he regarded one letter as important as the other. Can we safely hold that there was any inherent reason why one letter should be preserved and the other lost? Paul apparently had no expectation that one letter would be treasured for centuries bound in the same volume with the Law and the Prophets, and reverenced by the Christian world, while the other would be totally unknown save for this casual statement. There is, to be sure, a so-called "Epistle to the Laodiceans." But this document, which is found in Latin only, is repudiated by Christian scholars with the possible exception of Gregory the Great.

Paul had no conception of the Bible as we know it. Most likely he had no thought that he was furnishing a contribution to one of the sacred books of the world when he penned his friendly greetings to his far-away friends, or asked Timothy to hurry on to Rome with his cloak as winter was at hand, or when he asked a room and a bed of Philemon as he hoped soon to pay him a visit. In fact, the writings of the disciple of Jesus did not at once take rank with the Old Testament Scriptures. The early church fathers who quoted from the gospels deemed it necessary to supplement these quotations by the authority of the earlier writings. The New Testament did not at once come into its kingdom. The reverence we feel for it is not the result of any claim it has made, for itself of inerrancy or of inspiration. With the exception of a few guarded utterances it may be said to be remarkably silent as to its authority. Men have had more to say as to the proper attitude toward the New Testament than the New Testament itself.

As a completed volume we may say that the Bible is a human production. There were sacred Scriptures long before there was a sacred Book. The Spirit may have indited the Scriptures, but man made the Book. Whether the Book is larger or smaller than the Scriptures is a problem not as yet solved. The canon decides our relation toward the so-called sacred writings, and the canon is a human invention. That which has been rejected by this more or less arbitrary standard is stripped of authority, that which has been indorsed has thus received the official stamp of inspiration. And there is not yet an agreement upon this vital subject. The Council of Trent commits the Roman Catholic Church to much that is repudiated by Protestantism. Such and such sacred books inspired of God, according to one authority; these same books, according to another authority, but the product of human reason, unreliable and practically useless.

There is no proof that the canon of the Old Testament Scriptures had been settled in the time of Christ. In fact, the old manuscripts we possess of the Septuagint, the version used by Jesus and his disciples, contain much that is not acknowledged by Protestant authority to-day. Quotations are made in the apostolic writings from these discarded books.[1] As far as we know, it was to these books as well as to the more acceptable ones that Jesus referred when he said, "Ye search the Scriptures; . . . these are they which testify of me." The writings with which Timothy was familiar from childhood contained the books of Tobit, and Judith, and Susanna and the Dragon, and the like.

Moreover, the Old Testament contains quo-

[1] James 1. 19 from Ecclus. 5. 11; Rom. 9. 21 from Wisdom 15. 7

tations from many books that are not now supposed to be in existence. It is interesting to speculate as to the attitude of the Christian world toward these books should they be discovered—"The Book of Jasher," for instance, from which the brilliant quotation in reference to the standing of the sun upon Gibeon is made, or "The Book of the Wars of the Lord," in which was a record of what was done by the Lord in the Red Sea and in the brooks of Arnon (Num. 21. 14). Would the unearthing of these lost records mean a recasting of the canon, and a redraft of the Articles of Religion?

The New Testament as it stands is the result of centuries of discussion and conflict. Christian scholars and church councils at last have fixed its boundaries. That the Epistles of Clement, the Shepherd of Hermas, or the Apocalypse of Peter is not in the canon is not because of any inspired directions or order. These with others were circulated in the early days, and were regarded with more or less of reverence. The Sinaitic manuscript (fourth century) contains the Epistle of Barnabas. The Alexandrian Bible (fifth century) contains the Epistle of Clement, and in the table of contents refers to it under the head of

'Η ΚΑΙΝΗ ΔΙΑΘΗΚΗ.[1] Only by common consent and by the decision of councils have we the Bible of our day. Who now has the power to say that the book is too large or too small?

Thus has the great Book come to us, prepared at different times and under vastly differing circumstances; written by men who were strangers to each other, and without collusion or agreement as to purpose; then sifted by the slow process of time and the jealous scrutiny of criticism, until that which we have remains to us and we hold it as a precious gift from God.

Hence we meet with endless variety. The Book is a Joseph's coat of many colors, a treasure house in which is stored supplies for the world's need. Just what we want we may find here. High or low, rich or poor, learned or ignorant, all may come and be satisfied. There is history for the man who looks backward to the beginnings, and prophecy for him who looks forward into the to-morrow. There is prose for the sober and practical, and loftiest poetry for the imaginative and the dreamy. Are we looking for speculative philosophy? Let us try Ecclesiastes. Are we interested in sociology and political economy?

[1] Vincent, History of Textual Criticism, 20.

Here it is for us in Leviticus and Judges. Do we thrill at the touch of the heroic? Job, Esther, the Acts of the Apostles have material that will please. The Book runs the whole gamut of human need and human longing, even as its writers represent every grade of life and condition. The king is there writing with a golden stylus on the finest imported Egyptian papyrus; the shepherd penning his odes under the sky and in the midst of his sheep; the government official whose ready hand is accustomed to columns of figures and reports of trade; the physician studying the cases he must describe and giving us the benefit of his expert diagnosis; the fisherman who has not learned letters, who writes only because the mighty impulse has possessed him, and who would be more at home among the nets; the scholar trained to his work, skilled in the subtleties of speech, conversant with the best thought of others in the same field, and who "as occasion served would quote the choicest bits to enforce his own contention." Each man has given his best and the best of the age in which he lives. It is the gleaning of the ages. The sunshine of forty centuries purpling the vintage on a thousand hills is preserved in this sparkling wine. The great thoughts that ripened in the field of human endeavor and travail were in one generation gathered and stored with the thoughts of all preceding generations, and together they are bound into one sheaf and it stands for the richest fruitage of the human soul. Moses wrote the best that he knew, and Nehemiah indited his largest thoughts, and Paul gives us the essence of his age; each standing on tiptoe to get a broader horizon, and each profiting by all that had been said before him.

Thus we are ready to understand that which is manifest upon every page of the Book—that it is a growth. It gains in breadth and character as it rolls down the centuries. Uninspired religions do not improve. There is usually a manifest reversion to type. Mohammed hiding in the caves of Mecca proclaimed a purer faith than did Mohammed the master of men. The most ancient name given to God by one of the most ancient of faiths, Brahmanism, is "Dyaus-pitar," or Heaven-Father. This was simple and lofty and spiritual. But in the process of years this personal God became impersonal. Monotheism became materialism and pantheism. A hymn in the Egyptian "Book of the Dead," the oldest known literature in the world, speaks of God as the Self-existent One. The later religion of the Egyptian as known by the Greeks was gross and corrupt.

This recognized and universal law of deterioration has given the data by which many scholars claim to arrange the chronology of the Pentateuch. The laws of Israel are classified under four heads: 1. The Ten Words; 2. The Book of the Covenant; 3. The Deuteronomic Code; 4. The Levitical Codes. The Ten Words deal with that only which is fundamental. The Book of the Covenant is but an application of the Ten Words with its emphasis upon the one God and with its tacit indorsement of multiplied places of worship. The Deuteronomic Code, however, preserving the emphasis upon the unity of God, declares for one sanctuary, but without any special reference to the ritual. Then comes the Levitical Code, whose chief topic is the ritual. Hence it is claimed there is revealed a very marked deterioration. The Decalogue goes back to Moses. The Book of the Covenant may have been in existence 1000 B. C. The Deuteronomic Code was prepared in the days of Josiah; while Ezra and his associates are responsible for the Levitical Code. Let us accept this hypothetically; then the fact that this is not the trend of the entire series of revelations is strong presumptive proof that something has been at work besides the natural tendency to degeneration. We have received something better than the Levitical Code. The reversion to type, if such there be, has been checked. The Bible that lies on our table is a larger book than the Bible of the Temple and of Saint Paul. Not merely in size; not principally in size. Its light is clearer, its judgment is cleaner, its morals are purer. God did not say to the earlier writers what he said to those who came later. He did not teach the whole law in one lesson. It was daydawn before it was noon.

And so we find conditions in the older books that startle us and set us to wondering and explaining—actions that are contrary to our standards of right, and precepts that are outlawed by later revelations. The same voice that said to Israel, "Thou shalt love thy neighbor," said also, speaking of Ammon and Moab, "Because they met you not with bread and water in the way when ye came out of Egypt, and because they hired against thee Balaam to curse thee, . . . thou shalt not seek their peace nor their prosperity all thy days forever." And everybody knows what this language means when addressed to a nation of warriors already in the field. This same voice said later that this teaching was now out of date and the world was ready for another and a better code. "An eye for an eye, a tooth for a tooth," might do for Israel, crude, ignorant, debased; but such a creed received its death-blow on a later page of the same book; and this is the code of the savage only to-day. "The word spoken by angels was steadfast," let us believe, but it was inferior in character and authority to the "great salvation which at the first began to be spoken by the Lord and was confirmed with us by them that heard him."

Deborah the prophetess illustrates the age in which she lives. When Jael, the wife of Heber the Kenite, violates all the sacredness of hospitality and all the traditions of her sex by murdering the weary, unsuspecting Sisera, Deborah sings the exultant song:

"Blessed above women shall Jael be,
The wife of Heber the Kenite.
Blessed shall she be above women in the tent.
He asked water, she gave him milk;
She handed him cream in a dish of nobles.
She put her hand to the nail,
And her right hand to the workmen's hammer;
And hammered Sisera, broke his head,
And dashed in pieces and pierced his temples."

The vindictive prophetess even gloats over the desolation that has come to the far-away home of her enemy:

> "Through the window she looked forth and cried,
> The mother of Sisera through the lattice work;
> 'Why is his chariot so long in coming?
> Why tarry the steps of his team?'"

This act of Jael was the act of a savage squaw, and the exultation of Deborah was of no higher grade than the scalp dance of a victorious tribe decked with the trophies of a treacherous and heartless warfare. Such things would not be tolerated in these days because the later chapters of the same book have taught a nobler creed. The campaigns of Joshua, the imprecatory Psalms, the sacrifice of Jephthah, all these the world has outgrown and repudiated because the world has been taught by a riper revelation. Human lives are no longer to be shaped by these low standards and bloody precepts. This was significantly taught by Jesus. James and John, the sons of thunder, had studied the ancient methods; so when the villagers of Samaria refuse them hospitality they remembered the days of Elijah and asked if they too should call down fire from heaven. Then in a single sentence was shown the purpose of God: "Ye know not what manner of spirit ye are of. The Son of man is not come to destroy men's lives, but to save them." Not that there was rebuke to Elijah and his school. The spirit of this stern old reformer was ahead of his own age, and deserves praise only. It was rather a revelation of the fact that evolution had been at work, that "new occasions teach new duties, time makes ancient good uncouth." This new creed of the Master was vastly in advance of his own times, and the crucifixion was the result. It would have been entirely out of place and utterly helpless in the days of Elijah. The rocks must be blasted before the temple is built, and this can be done by force only. The ore must be melted before the vessels of honor may be fashioned, and this is the work of fire.

Perhaps the simplest way to illustrate the growth of revelation would be by a summary of life as it is operated upon by divine influences. Take, for instance, the life of Jacob. He is sufficiently crude and primitive at the outset, and his case makes an interesting study. There are three periods in his life as affected by the supernatural: First, when asleep in his enforced exile from home, in a dream the ladder appears, the angels descending and ascending, and he calls the place Beth-el, or "the House of God." Again, when returning from Haran after his separation from Laban the angels of God meet him, and he calls the place of meeting Mahanaim, or "the Hosts of God." And, finally, when he wrestles all night with his mysterious visitor, he calls the place Peniel, or "the Face of God." Here is a regular evolution. At first only a dream in the slumbers of the night, and the angels moved on their errands regardless of his presence. It was only the House of God, general, indefinite, open to the world. In the second instance he saw the messengers of God when he was wide-awake. They met him on his journey. They came at a time of great uncertainty and suspense. The defrauded Laban had been placated, but what guarantee was there of safety from the defrauded Esau. The epiphany of the angelic hosts seemed to relate to this, seemed to hold somewhere and somehow a solution of this problem. But still it was ambiguous. It was without the personal touch. As in the earlier appearance, it was by inference only that he could connect the vision with his own need; the inference now, however, was vastly stronger and clearer. The third instance is the climax. Here was no dream, and no casual meaning. There could be no question as to the import of this manifestation. It is now Peniel, the Face of God. It is while broadly awake and with every faculty alert. Moreover, now the supernatural factor is not oblivious and self-centered as in the first interview; not remote and ambiguous as in the second. The purpose of God has been striding forward, and in his giant grip does the Angel hold the Man until the daybreak softens the peaks of Gilead and the waking camp on the other side of Jabbok begins to shiver in the mists of the morning.

Take another illustration, and one that sweeps a wider segment and touches more closely the common heart. It is well known that the Old Testament does not commit itself on the subject of immortality and the future life. Israel was content with promises of material good. Long life, posterity as the sands of the sea, the fruit of the vine and the product of the olive press—this was the range of their eschatological dreams. There are references and allusions more or less definite. We find such expressions as, "He was gathered to his fathers," or "to his people." We are told that the "body must return to the earth from whence it was taken, but the spirit to God who gave it," a text which may easily be made to do service in defense of the doctrine of absorption. The doctrine of immortality as we have it to-day may be said to have grown with the growth of the Book. Let us look at this development.

In the earliest days Enoch passes away. It is all obscure, and the sacred writer does not attempt to remove the obscurity. Perhaps he is unable to remove it. Perhaps he writes all he knows. The patriarch in question "was," and then he "was not," and the only plausible explanation is that "God took him." It seems to be an exception to the general rule. Something mysterious has occurred. Case after case had been cited. Lives had been lived, children had been begotten, and then in every instance the matter closed by the short, swift sentence, "and he died." From Adam to Noah it had been easy to write the biography. There was no eccentricity; there was no challenge. The world walked in a beaten track, and the work of the historian was simple. But with Enoch came the first divergence. He could not be classified. He did not die as others had died, and so is noted the great exception, and in bewilderment the historian writes, "He was not, for God took him." Thus was spoken the first parable, and it is the beginning of the story of the triumph of life over death. The first faint streaks of the dawn that shall some day flood the cemeteries of the world.

Somewhat later and the second object lesson is given. Moses is to be taken away. He is to die. At any rate, it is supposed that he is to die, but again there is mystery. No eye is to look upon him as he passes away, and no human being is to know where the body lies. The people know only when the event is to occur, and they are permitted to watch the venerable figure move up the mountain side and disappear down the slope that looks toward Canaan. The great solution has moved a step nearer. Then comes the case of Elijah. He too is taken hence. Now indeed the agency of his translation is seen and the phenomenon noted, because at last one man has been found ready to receive the mighty revelation. It does not yet belong to the world. The shadows are still somber and chill in the valleys; but there are gleams on the high places, and one man is able to catch the flash of the heavenly chariots because he of all the race has climbed to these high places. Elijah's translation was a stage in the evolution of revealed truth, and

Elisha's power of vision was a stage in the evolution of the race. Some such ascension and translation occurred in each of the other cases, perhaps, but there was no one to see. The world was not trained to see; it was not ready and able to see.

The climax is reached when the new dispensation was inaugurated. The God-Man came to bring immortality to light. It was his plan to give the finished lesson to the now prepared race. He would lift the curtain and let the inner glory flash out upon the world. Man now was able to witness the whole process. Calmly and deliberately the great Demonstrator submitted to death and was buried. Care was taken that the work be thorough, and testimony to the decease was filed. There must be no flaw in the experiment. Then on Easter morning came the demonstration. Amid the shaking of the earthquake an angel appeared and rolled away the stone from the door of the sepulcher, and, behold, the sepulcher was empty. And the risen Christ walked among men and was seen of many. The great revelation was complete. It had taken thirty centuries for its unfolding. Enoch and Moses and Elijah and Christ: this was the story in chapters; this was the dynasty of development, until the zenith is reached and the scholar of Tarsus is ready to write in large, full characters, "For we know that if our earthly house of this tabernacle were dissolved we have a building of God, an house not made with hands, eternal in the heavens."

These are only sidelights and suggest the general trend. The Book itself is a history of redemption, and of the Redeemer. In Genesis the curse is pronounced, in the Revelation we are told of a time or a state in which "there shall be no more curse." In Genesis the race is driven from the tree of life, and a flaming sword guards the gateway. In the Revelation we are told that the leaves of this tree are for the healing of the nations. In Genesis the serpent-symbol of evil makes his appearance and his track is seen down through the book. In the Revelation this old serpent is cast into the lake of fire and humanity is forever freed from his machinations. The garden of the first book, suggestive of primitive days and simple lives, is transformed into the city of the last book, the exponent of modern conditions, and that which has been prepared for one family is succeeded by that which shall be the home of redeemed and enlightened nations.

What a marvelous evolution it is, and how divinely it is inspired and managed, while through it one supreme, majestic figure moves, the reason for it all, the explanation of it all, the glory of it all! Coming into view on its very first pages; growing in distinctness and increasing in prominence until he steps into the clear light of the newest dispensation, and, lo! "the Word was made flesh, and dwelt among us, and we beheld his glory as of the only begotten of the Father, full of grace and truth."

XII

EPILOGUE

XII

Epilogue

WE no longer fear the argument of the atheist nor the sneers of the scoffer. No one tries to demonstrate that Jesus is a myth, or that Christianity is a cunningly devised fable. Skepticism of that type is as old-fashioned and as amusing as the lumbering stage coach or the clumsy firelocks of the fathers. There is, however, a spirit of materialism abroad in the land. Our books, our newspapers, our pulpits are filled with figures and progress and scientific discoveries. This is emphatically the Zeitgeist, and is in line of succession from the past. From the days of prehistoric man through all the bloody centuries to Constantine physical force was paramount. The world was a cage of wild beasts. The spoil was to the strongest. There was no pity and there was no help. Nation rushed against nation in the howling maelstrom of war. What a great rude, clumsy, murderous animal was man, inventing new deaths for his fellow man and marking new boundary lines on the map with blood.

Then came Constantine, whose arm was strong, it is true, but whose cunning was masterful. He would teach the race a new game, and create new reasons for men to hate each other. So he played upon human passions, he appealed to latent superstition, he united church and state and pledged the assistance of an almighty hand in their cruelties and slaughter. Ecclesiasticism ruled from Constantine to Galileo, and its record is the slime track of the snail across the arid plains of the Middle Ages. The church listened at every keyhole, sat in the university chairs, and forbade the earth to move because it did not believe in movement or progress of any kind. But the telescope came, and the printing press, and the railroads, and the power of the dead hand was broken and there obtained a new alignment of ideas and forces. And what now? What but a pitiful materialism that exalts the stuff, glorifies the ponderable, and that tends to strangle the noblest instincts of the soul. We measure our evolution as a people, our enlargement as individuals, in terms of the invoice book or the market place. There are so many millions of population this year against so many last year, so many battleships in the navy as compared with the navy of Germany or of Japan, hence we are fulfilling our national destiny. Our bank account is plus instead of minus, at any rate let us say that it is hypothetically, hence our life has been a success. We have canal locks that could lift the Kaiser Wilhelm der Grosse to the top of a mountain. We have grown impatient of the measureless waste at Niagara, and now the world's wonder is beginning to turn the world's wheels and to grind flour for the world's bread. We have calculated in foot-pounds the energy expended in driving the earth along its swift path among the stars, and no doubt would like to hitch the whole machinery to our dynamos and advertise "power to let."

This trend is seen in our educational methods. Where once the boys and girls studied with persistent emphasis classic poetry and ancient love songs they now study the use of tools and the analysis of the soil. Once the schools dealt in ideas, now they concern themselves with gases and minerals. Once the children learned to parse sonorous sentences from Milton, or to paraphrase the stately periods of Addison, or to translate the war songs of Homer; now all this divides the time with the fermenting process in baking a loaf of bread, or the amount of energy in a pound of anthracite coal. What did our fathers know about geology? What did they care? The earth was a derelict world and would soon be destroyed; why study so ephemeral an object? Astronomy is but a few years out of the nursery. Martin Luther said of Copernicus, "This fool wishes to reverse the entire science of astronomy." Sir Isaac Newton's theory of gravitation was held to "dethrone Providence." Charles Darwin when a boy was publicly rebuked by the head master at Shrewsbury for wasting his time on such a useless subject as chemistry. His nickname in the school was "Gas," and in the vigorous though not very elegant phraseology of the playground the despised science of chemistry was known as "stinks." Now these sciences are familiar to the children; they are taught in the crossroad schoolhouse; they have taken front rank in the college curriculum.

Our modern science is looking for facts, and facts are popular nowadays. It does not care where they are to be found, nor concern itself with the effects of the discovery. It wants facts. It has no time for sentiment; it is impatient of preaching; it has no taste for beauty. It overturns with ruthless hand our

Epilogue

nursery ideas as to the beginnings of things, and pushing its investigations back it finds, or it professes to find, or it is entirely willing to find, the origin of the human race in the locomotive larva of a compound ascidian, disporting itself in the slimy ooze of the prehistoric sea; one of whose offspring set out like Abram from Ur with its face toward the future and the incipient instincts and aspirations of humanity beating in its sluggish pulses. It traces the teeming universe back to an original star dust drifting through uncharted space. It has no place for what it cannot see; it does not know spirit; it does not need God. This is Physical Science, a lusty Titan called from the vasty deep and led out into the light during the last century. When reverent and modest it becomes another Columbus leading to new and splendid worlds; when irreverent and reckless it is Phaëthon driving the chariot of the sun with untried hands and bringing darkness and disaster.

This influence is seen in our ideas of sanitation. There was a time when disease was supposed to be caused by evil spirits; when physical disorders were to be cured by prayer, or the touch of the king, or contact with the relics of a saint. The bones of Saint Rosalie at Palermo healed scores of devotees. A meddling scientist discovered that they were the bones of a goat; they went right on, however, with undiminished healing power. An exorcism in Latin was the best thing to stop an epidemic, and a prayer meeting would break up a fever. We are learning better things nowadays. The Scotch clergymen who petitioned Lord Palmerston to appoint a day of fasting and prayer on account of the cholera were told to go home and clean their streets. "God give you better health—and more sense," said William of Orange to the patient who pleaded for the king's touch. We are preaching the gospel of good drainage. We call the evil spirits microbes, and instead of vaticination after mediæval precedent our modern prophets are given to vaccination. This is a move in the right direction, and the world is cleaner and healthier therefor. Yet there is always danger that the pendulum, once aswing, will swing too far. There is a soul, though the surgeons do not find it with their knives and their microscopes, and everything of this world and of the next depends upon how we regard and cultivate that soul. There are evil spirits, though that which our fathers called possession may sometimes have been hysteria. We are pushing back the limits of the supernatural; we are invading its territory, or that which once seemed to be its territory. We are touching with our lancets the very sources of life, but let us remember that the secrets are not all told yet. The atom of life which the biologist is watching on the stage of his microscope contains that within its tiny cells which links it with eternity, which baffles research, which sits in quiet scorn waiting for him to announce what it is, and whence it comes, and whither it moves in the orbit of its occult existence.

Even our philanthropies are caught in the swing of this tide. Never has there been such marked solicitude in reference to the physical. The latest charge against intemperance is that it destroys muscle and disintegrates brain tissue. The violent upheaval against tenement houses is based upon material issues. Disease comes through these insanitary conditions, and the next generation will be handicapped and the stamina of the race weakened. And so we are told how many families have been visited, how many sick children cared for, how many city-smitten wretches sent into the country on fresh-air tickets. This is a hopeful sign. These bodies are the temple of the Holy

Ghost. The Word was made flesh and dwelt among us. The best way so often to minister to a mind diseased is to begin with the diseased body. But again I say when once we are started in any given direction it is so hard to stop, or even to slow down. Monomania is unbalanced mental inertia. Error lies so hard upon the territory of truth that it is never more than a few days' journey off in any direction we may be facing.

Thus we are beginning to settle the profoundest questions of ethics with physical counters. Judas Iscariot, we are told, was imperfectly nourished when a child, hence his treason when he grew to man's estate. Nero had a clot of blood pressing upon his brain. The murderer of President McKinley was but obeying the impulses of some savage ancestor when he plunged the nation into grief. Heredity and environment, we have made these our scapegoats, and on them have laid the sins of this generation. Conscience is the half-forgotten voice of some one who spoke to us in the cradle. Morality is the harmonious adjustment of the brain molecules. Religion is an instinct begotten of the ghost stories told about the forest fires by our wandering semi-simian ancestors.

Epilogue

"Son of man, can these dry bones live? Can this glorious age be rescued from the blight of spiritual paralysis? How shall we bring new life to these dry bones, and clothe them anew with supple muscles and with tingling nerves? Only by a recrudescence of the supernatural; by a new vision of the divine immanence; by a renewed uncovering of the hiding place of power. We have been misplacing the emphasis on the startling words, "With God all things are possible"—so misplacing it, indeed, that a great truth is liable to become a great falsehood. There are impossibilities to God. He cannot make our life; he cannot mar it. This text does not imply centralization, but coöperation. God alone cannot do the impossible, neither can we; but you and I *with* God and the impossible ceases to be.

There is no success without this alliance. The musician may seek to ignore God. He may say, "I am looking for new chords and richer combinations, and God has nothing to do with it." And so he tries over and over the changing harmonies until by and by he cries out, "I have it, I have it! It is something new; it will make me famous; the world has never heard the like before." But it is one of

God's old chords, harmonized from the foundation of time, and sung by the morning stars on the daydawn of history. And it is when a Haydn can voice the crash of storm or the roll of thunder in his "Creation," or a Beethoven can reproduce the ripple of waves and the rustle of leaves in his "Moonlight Sonata"—God's storms and God's waves—it is then that the people are thrilled. The artist succeeds only as he works with God. He may shut himself up in his studio, and mix his paints and blunder along with his petty conceptions, and nobody cares; but when a Moran goes to the Yellowstone and catches the glory of the Falls and the Cañon; when a Turner puts the blazing morning sky in his Ulysses and Polyphemus, or a group of pines, a running stream, and a distant glimpse of the sea, in his "Crossing the Brook"—it is then, when God steps upon the canvas, that men take off their hats and stand in awe.

It is the coming of the Christ into human life, into daily life, into professional life, that is to mean sanity and success. Just as Paul of Tarsus met the artistic materialism of Athens by preaching Jesus and the resurrection; just as Martin Luther met the ecclesiastical materialism of the dark ages by thundering the old doctrines of repentance toward God and faith toward our Lord Jesus Christ; just as John Wesley, and Rowland Hill, and John Fletcher met the deistic materialism of the eighteenth century by a return to first principles and a reaffirmation of the supreme facts of the spiritual, as illustrated in the life, death, and resurrection of Jesus of Nazareth, and the Spirit witness of spiritual life in the believer's heart.

We are more than body. There is more than the visible. The world is more than laws. There was something before yesterday; there will be something after to-morrow. The dear dead forms that lie so still and tranquil in the casket will not lie mute and unresponsive forever. They are not "drowned in the depths of a meaningless past." They will live again, and they will smile again, when we touch their hands on the eternal hills. Let us be reverent, let us be humble, let us be exultant. There is reason for our faith; there is reason in our faith. We are not machines, cash registers, beasts of burden. In the supreme moment when man became a living soul he was differentiated from the tribes that move upon the earth's surface or swim in its seas. His forehead in that moment was lifted to the divine level, his feet were turned into the King's highway that leads through the eternities.

Two boats are out yonder fishing side by side. Presently the anchors are lifted and they start for home. One fisherman puts out his oars and pulls sturdily toward the shore. The other seems to drift; he ships no oars; he makes no haste. He is lifting into the air a broad white piece of canvas. It is not ornamental, it affords no screen from the sun, it is apparently useless. But presently it is fixed in its place; then it grows rigid, there is a straining of stays, a swaying of spars, and now away flies the boat, flinging the white spray from her prow and hastening to the land. The first boat is a fish, the second boat is a bird. One gets its power from below, the other from above. One lives in the world of the visible, the slow, the commonplace; the other has reached out into the invisible, has taken hold of the unseen. What opportunities there are above us! What a world of majesty and breadth is there! We do not see it, we cannot understand it, but we have endowments and affinities which, like the spread sail of the boatman, adjust themselves to this glorious spiritual realm and bear us as on wings. Let us get up our sails. The winds are blowing over land and sea. They are blowing seaward. All down the horizon great ships are sailing. Mighty spiritual fleets are out there, sailing, sailing, over an ocean wide as eternity and sunlit with the gracious smile of God. "The glorious company of the apostles, the goodly fellowship of the prophets, the noble army of martyrs," all these have entered into communion with the invisible, have set their affections upon the spiritual, have touched the pulse of the Infinite.

"I came that they may have life, and that they may have abundance," is the latest word. It is the newest and the surest promise of hope for to-day. "And the stretching out of his wings shall fill the breadth of the land, O Immanuel."

INDEX

INDEX

A

Abraham........PAGE 91
Adam................ 55
Adamite, Daughters of. 60
Æschylus............ 182
Ages of the world...... 219
Agnosticism........... 83
Alexandrian manuscript 248
Ambrose............. 213
Amherst............. 193
Anglo-Saxon.......... 62
Apatheia............. 20
Apostolic times........ 226
Aquinas, Thomas...... 79
Arbitration, Court of... 112
Archangel, Guido Reni's 186
Arminius, James...... 143
Artists and Christ..... 214
Aryan............... 62
Astronomy...127, 209, 220
Athenians............ 56
Atonement retroactive. 64

B

Baptism...........86, 139
Baptist, John the...... 81
Barbarians........... 95
Bartholomew, Saint... 131
Beth-el.............. 257
Bible.............160, 239
Biography............ 93
"Book of Dead"...... 251
Brewster, Sir David.... 65
Brooks, Phillips....... 34
Brotherhood of man... 56

Browning...PAGE 130, 211
Buddha.............19, 88
Butler's Analogy...... 162
Byron............... 60

C

Cain................ 59
Caliban............. 130
Calvinism........... 141
Canon, Old Testament.. 247
Canterbury, Archbishop of................ 73
Capital and labor..... 231
Capuchins, Church of.. 186
Carboniferous Era..... 188
Cathedrals........... 44
Cave men........... 60
Charlemagne........93, 219
Charles V........... 140
Chemistry........... 270
Chemosh............ 136
Chrysostom.......... 79
Church, Institutional.. 44
Classification........ 73
Clement............. 248
Coleridge............ 84
Colossians........... 245
Columbus........... 39
Commerce........... 119
Communism......... 230
Confucius........... 88
Constantine......... 268
Covenant, Book of.197, 252
Creeds, Necessary.... 203
Criticism............ 80

Cromwell........PAGE 219
Cross.....85, 179, 188, 192
Crusaders............ 228

D

Damascus, Great Mosque of................. 157
Dante................ 139
Darwin, Charles. 14, 72, 270
Deborah.............. 254
Declaration of Independence................. 184
Design, Argument from 163
Dispensations, The..... 220
Disraeli.............. 210
Divorce.............. 233
Doctrines............. 200
Drummond........14, 189

E

Edom................ 33
Education............. 269
Egyptians..........56, 241
Election.............. 141
Elijah...........256, 260
Emancipation Proclamation.............. 116
Enoch................ 259
Environment.......... 45
Ephraim, Son of....... 184
Epictetus............. 205
Epicurus.............. 95
Esarhaddon........... 130
Ethics................ 274
Ethnology............ 58
Evangelist's picture of Christ............... 214
Evolution............. 14
Ezekiel............... 224

F

Family, The.......... 233
Fiske, John........... 190

Flood..........PAGE 59
Froebel.............. 142
Fuegians............. 72

G

Gabriel............... 240
Gardiner, Allen....... 72
Genesis.....58, 60, 209, 262
Geology..........209, 270
George, Saint......... 187
German emperor...... 122
Gideon............... 224
Gods, Local.......... 41
Gracchi and Moses.... 213
Greeks............... 177

H

Hamilton, Alexander.. 118
Harnack.............. 80
Hawthorne.........13, 186
Hegel................ 12
Heredity............. 45
Hexateuch............ 241
History.............. 114
Hobbes............... 26
Homer............... 178
Honoratus............ 39
Hosea................ 199
Hospital, Charity...... 92
Howe, Julia Ward..... 123
Hughes, Hugh Price... 166
Humane, Survival of the 193
Humanity, Gospel of... 48
Huxley............... 22

I

Immortality in Old Testament.............. 258
Incas, The............ 105
Indians and smallpox... 193
Industrialism......... 228
Intellect, Selfish....... 25
Isaiah............33, 183

Iscariot, Judas....PAGE 274
Israel.............57, 136

J

Jacob.............130, 256
Japanese creation...... 56
Jehovah.............. 223
Jephtha.............. 136
Jethro's daughters..... 206
Joshua............128, 255
Judges............... 241

K

Kant................. 68
Kennicott............ 80
Khan, Grand......... 36
Khayyan, Omar......85, 157
Kidd, Benjamin....... 189
Kingdom of God...154, 156, 232
Kipling, Rudyard...... 115
Knights of the Cross... 140
Koornhert............ 143

L

Lanier, Sidney.....156, 208
Laodicea, Epistle to... 245
Leibnitz............. 80
Lenormant........... 58
Lessing.............. 80
Life, Value of........ 89
Lincoln.............. 50
Linnæus............. 73
Logos............... 85
Lowell, James R....... 182
Luther, Martin.....219, 276

M

Mahanaim............ 257
Mandeville, Sir John... 161
Marcus Aurelius....... 205
Markham, Edwin...... 229

Mars' Hill........PAGE 57
Materialism.......210, 267
Mazdean............. 37
Menes............... 56
Mexico, Princes of..... 131
Midgard serpent....183, 207
Milton............... 51
Miriam, Hawthorne's.. 186
Missionaries.......... 38
Mohammed.......240, 251
Moses....130, 197, 206, 208, 211, 223, 240, 260
Mount, Sermon on..... 204
Muller, Max.......... 37
Mythology........... 69

N

Napoleon............. 193
Nature.......168, 171, 188
Nero................. 274
Nile................. 136
Nirvana............. 19
Normans............. 62

O

Odin................. 134
Opportunism......... 231
Oracle, Delphian...... 183
Osiris............... 94

P

Palmerston, Lord...... 272
Patriotism........... 102
Pantheon............. 135
Paul of Tarsus.....57, 226, 245, 276
Peace Congress....108, 235
Peniel............... 257
Pentecost............ 154
Pestalozzi........... 142
Peter and Ananias..... 230
Philanthropy.... 230, 273
Philip and Greeks..... 177

Philip, Commodore PAGE 194
Philo.................. 85
Plagues, Egyptian..... 136
Pliny's classification... 73
Poe's Raven........... 26
Pompeii............... 185
Pope, Alexander....... 192
Prodigal Son...50, 147, 203
Prometheus............ 181
Property..........120, 228
Puritan............... 79

R

Raleigh, Sir Walter.... 40
Religion............68, 190
Republics............. 118
Resurrection of Christ.. 261
Revolution, War of the. 115
Rossetti.............. 129
Rousseau, Contrat Social................ 142
Russell, Lord.......... 111

S

Salisbury, Lord........ 121
Samiasa............... 60
Samuel................ 131
Sanitation, Modern.... 271
Science..........24, 92, 270
Sepoy rebellion........ 110
Servant of Jehovah.... 183
Shakespeare........50, 118
Sienkiewicz............ 140
Sierra, Leone.......... 71
Sinai.................. 200
Sinaitic manuscript.... 248
Sistine Chapel......... 144
Socialism.............. 234
Soul, Growth of...153, 169, 172
Sparta................ 119
Spencer, Herbert...... 104
Spinoza............... 80
Spiritual life.......... 277
Supper, The Great..... 42

T

Taft, William H..PAGE 104
Tennyson...........18, 106
Theological seminaries.. 202
Theology, Opposition to 201
Thor...............86, 134
Thug, Indian.......... 67
Tobit, Book of........ 247
Trent, Council of...140, 247
Troy.................. 178
Turanian.............. 62

U

Universe..........127, 128

V

Valhalla.............. 134
Valjean, Jean......... 66
Van Dyke, Henry..... 228
Vedas................. 18
Venezuela............. 121
Vertebrata............ 74
Vespasian............. 226

W

Wallace, Alfred Russell. 190
Washington, George, at Yorktown........... 194
Wesley, John......144, 277
Westward Ho.......... 159
Whittier, "Eternal Goodness".......... 132
Wolseley, Lord........ 105

X

Xavier, Francis....... 40

Z

Zion Redeemed........ 183

WITHDRAWN
from
Funderburg Library